Early Greek Lyric Poetry

Early Greek Lyric Poetry

Translated with an Introduction and Commentary

David Mulroy

Ann Arbor

THE UNIVERSITY OF MICHIGAN PRESS

First paperback edition 1999
Copyright © by the University of Michigan 1992
All rights reserved
Published in the United States of America by
The University of Michigan Press
Manufactured in the United States of America

2002   2001   4   3   2

Library of Congress Cataloging-in-Publication Data

Early Greek lyric poetry / translated with an introduction and
    commentary [by] David Mulroy.
        p. cm.
    Includes bibliographical references and index.
    ISBN 0-472-10296-6 (alk. paper)
    1. Greek poetry—Translations into English.   I. Mulroy, David D.,
    1943–   .
PA3622.M85   1992
884′.0108—dc20   91-42973
                                                            CIP

ISBN 0-472-08606-5 (pbk)

For Mary, Cecily, and Travis

Acknowledgments

I was enabled to do my first serious work on translating Greek poetry by an Undergraduate Teaching Improvement Grant from the University of Wisconsin System during the summer of 1988. Colleagues and students in Milwaukee, especially Laura Barnard and Eugene Jones, gave me much valuable encouragement and advice, as did Mary Lamprecht of the University of California Press. I am most grateful to Ellen Bauerle of the University of Michigan Press for deciding to take this project on and to her, her associates at the Press, and the scholars whom she enlisted as anonymous referees for their courteous and helpful guidance and criticism.

Map 1. Mainland Greece, Thrace, and the Cycladic Islands

Map 2. Lydia and the Ionian Islands (modern Turkey)

Contents

Contents

Introduction

In the eighth century B.C., the Greek poet Hesiod thought that he lived in mankind's worst age, on the edge of civilization's self-destruction (*Works and Days* 174–201). In fact, he was at the beginning of an era of remarkable progress. Between 750 and 500 B.C., the Hellenic world blossomed into an array of vibrant city-states, whose achievements in many fields were to set standards for centuries to come. We have no contemporary historical account of this period, but much of its poetry survives. The earliest examples are Homer's epics and Hesiod's didactic poems, which were probably composed in the eighth century. The works of both poets consist of dactylic hexameter verse, which was recited by individuals. The seventh and sixth centuries are represented by the earlier Homeric Hymns—mythological narratives in the Homeric style and meter—and a number of other poems that vary widely in meter and topic. Of these some were meant to be sung by individuals, others by choruses; still others were chanted or merely recited by individuals. Though not strictly logical, the term "lyric poetry" is often used to distinguish these works from those in dactylic hexameter. Except for an anthology traditionally attributed to Theognis, the lyric poetry of these two centuries survives only in fragments: either literal fragments of ancient papyrus or excerpts preserved as quotations in later authors. This volume contains a translation of a comprehensive selection of the fragments of early Greek lyric poetry together with highlights from the Theognidean anthology. To round out the picture, selections from the works of the lyric poets of the early fifth century, Bacchylides and Pindar, and the principal fragments of Pindar's supposed female rival, Corinna, have also been included.

Historical Background I: From Mycenae to the Archaic Period

The ultimate origins of the first Greeks, the Mycenaeans, are not known. Most scholars think that they were nomads who entered

Greece from the north about 1900 B.C. and gradually developed an advanced bronze-age civilization under the influence of the Cretans and Egyptians. What *is* known on the basis of archaeology is that by 1600 the mainland was dominated by Greek-speaking kings who lived in impressive citadels in Mycenae, Tiryns, Pylos, and elsewhere and were wealthy enough to be buried in golden funeral masks. To help administer their surprisingly complex bureaucracies, they employed scribes who kept official records in the "Linear B" syllabary, the earliest surviving form of Greek writing. Clay tablets with Linear B on them were accidentally preserved at the end of the period when the buildings that housed them were destroyed by fire. The discovery of Linear B tablets in the ruins of the palace of Cnossus on the island of Crete has led scholars to infer that the Mycenaeans conquered that kingdom, the realm of the legendary Minos, about 1450. By 1250, the Mycenaeans had built a prosperous, cohesive society, which included most of the Peloponnesus, the Isthmus, Attica, Boeotia, parts of Thessaly, many of the Aegean islands, and possibly Miletus on the Turkish coast.

The Greeks were divided into tribal groups differentiated by dialect and custom. Most influential were the Ionians and the Dorians. The rulers of the Mycenaean centers in the Peloponnesus were ancestors of the Ionians. The Dorians, on the other hand, originally lived in north, in Thessaly and northwestern Greece. It is possible that they were the people who began making raids on the Mycenaean centers in the south towards the end of the thirteenth century. Whoever the raiders were, they eventually destroyed the palaces and forced their rulers to scatter. During this troubled time Mycenaeans sacked the city of Troy, near the Hellespont—an intrinsically minor event that became the great Trojan War of legend.[1] After the destruction of the Mycenaean palaces, Dorians, who may or may not have been the destroyers, occupied the Peloponnesus. Hence the whole sequence of events is sometimes referred to as the "Dorian invasion."

The collapse of Mycenae marked the beginning of a dark age. There is no more evidence of large-scale buildings or Linear B writing. Pottery was crude, trade depressed, communities very small.[2] Several developments, however, laid the foundation for the rapid recovery that was to come. One was a series of migrations from the Greek mainland. The Mycenaeans had already occupied some Aegean islands and sites on the Turkish coast. Around 1000 B.C., they consolidated control of the coast. Happily for them, the sudden collapse of the Hittite empire, which happened at the same time as the "Dorian Invasion," had left the area in a political vacuum. Traditionally, the first migrations were led by Aeolians from Boeotia and Thessaly. Greek cities on Lesbos were established or strengthened, others rose on the coast south of the great island. The most prosperous of these was Cumae, where Hesiod's father once lived.

The Ionian cities were south of the Aeolian ones. Athens is said to have organized the Ionian migration, and it would have been in a position to do so since it was the only important Mycenaean center not destroyed by raiders. Refugees from the south, especially from King Nestor's Messenian realm, came to Athens, then sailed east to found new homes: Ephesus, Chios, Samos, and the others. Miletus may have been Greek already; if not, it became so now.

The Dorians also extended their power across the Aegean. They occupied Mycenaean settlements on the southern islands of Melos, Thera, Rhodes, and Cos, and founded new cities on the coast, Cnidus and Halicarnassus.

Another positive factor consisted of one of the greatest inventions of all time: the Greek alphabet. This resulted from collaboration between Greeks and Phoenicians. The earliest scripts were syllabaries, in which each sign stood for a whole syllable: PA, TE, KI, etc. Syllabaries were bulky; for example, there were over eighty signs in Linear B. They were also inexact, being unable to represent final consonants. The Phoenician script used during the Greek dark age was an improvement. It contained only twenty-two signs, all standing for consonants; vowels had to be guessed. Some ambiguity resulted but the script was easy to learn, and it is said that the Phoenicians themselves had begun to write some vowels separately.

The Greeks borrowed Phoenician letters to represent equivalent consonants in their own tongue. Consonant signs that seemed superfluous were used for vowels. Phoenician aleph, for example, a smooth breathing mark, became alpha, standing for *ah*. Given a full set of vowels, the consonant signs no longer stood for actual syllables but for consonants in the abstract: positionings of the lips and tongue at the beginning or end of vowel sounds. In this way, a simple, unambiguous method of recording speech was born.[3]

It is not known whether the alphabet was invented all at once or evolved over a period of years.[4] One way or the other, it was being widely used early in the eighth century. There is an attractive theory that the alphabet was devised specifically to record poetry.[5] Some of the earliest alphabetic inscriptions contain verse, which could not be accurately represented without separate signs for vowels and consonants.

Dark-age Greeks may well have wanted a way to record poetry, because an unusually rich tradition of oral poetry was evolving among them. At its heart were stories about the Mycenaeans, and historical truth was greatly diluted. What took shape was a fantastic picture of wealthy kings and their mighty armies as imagined by storytellers in a humble agrarian society. Hovering over the heroes was a family of anthropomorphic deities with more than their share of human foibles. At first the artists who created and preserved this tradition were oral poets, masters of memory. In their own minds, they were probably only repeating what they had heard from older poets, with an occasional assist from the Muse; in fact they were molding skillful fictions. Somehow such performances crystallized in the monumental *Iliad* and *Odyssey*. It is not known whether either or both were actually the work of a single poet or what role, if any, writing had in the design of the poems. Later tradition attributed them to "Homer." If the alphabet was not invented to help create or preserve them, its fortuitous appearance just in time to do so was an amazing coincidence.

The other known poet of the eighth century was Hesiod, the author of *Theogony* and *Works and Days*. In his poems, Hesiod describes himself as a farmer in central Greece. His father had attempted to settle in the Aeolian colony of Cumae, but had had to return to the mainland because of financial difficulties. Whereas Homer told stories in which catalogs were sometimes inserted, Hesiod did the reverse: *Theogony* enumerates the Greek gods according to genealogy; *Works and Days* lists the jobs that a farmer should do during the year. Of the inserted narratives, some are famous. We owe to Hesiod the story of the castration of Uranus and birth of Aphrodite from the sea; also, those of Pandora and Prometheus, and the descent of man from the primordial golden age to the awful iron age of the present.

Greek civilization made a remarkable recovery starting in the middle of the eighth century, about the time that Hesiod foretold its end. The invention of the alphabet and the literacy it fostered may have been a factor; the broader political context was certainly one. The fall of Mycenae had been part of a general instability in the eastern Mediterranean. Not only did the Hittite empire vanish, the Egyptians were kept from the Mediterranean by the marauding Peoples of the Sea, a throng that included displaced Greeks and Israelites. Unsettled conditions lasted for four centuries until the Assyrians emerged as the dominant power in the near east. Critical to their success was a series of battles in the second half of the eighth century, by which they established military supremacy on the Syrian coast of the Mediterranean.

The emergence of an imperial power meant increasing stability and trade.[6] Greek cities established during the age of migration prospered under improved conditions. Smyrna, an Aeolian settlement that was taken over by Ionians, has been thoroughly studied by archaeologists. It seems to have grown from a tiny village to a congested city, with a population of about 3,000 at the end of the eighth century.[7] Aristotle says that most of the citizens of neighboring Colophon were wealthy in the eighth century and owned extensive property (*Politics* 1290b). Xenophanes adds that at least a thousand of them came to assembly wearing purple robes, a sign of wealth (fragment 5 in this volume). Trade alone cannot explain this affluence. Apparently, the Greek settlers managed to exploit the labor of Asiatic natives on their farms. It was in such cities that the singers who created the Homeric poems perfected their art. If there ever was a "Homer," a good guess is that he came from Smyrna.[8]

A second round of Greek expansion began in the eighth century. The new colonies, like the old, were independent of their mother cities and were a result of overpopulation. Typical colonists were farmers in search of new soil, and they were numerous and energetic. City-states sprang up all around the Mediterranean region from Marseilles in the west to the eastern shore of the Black Sea; there was even a settlement of Greek soldiers in the Egyptian desert.[9] One of the earliest colonies was founded by the Euboean cities of Chalchis and Eretria on the island of Ischia in the Bay of Naples. Known as Pithecusae, this site has yielded some of the earliest Greek inscriptions. One is particularly memorable. It was recovered from a shattered drinking cup, which was manufactured in Rhodes and buried with its owner about 720. In book 11 of the *Iliad*, lines 631–36, Homer describes an unusually large and ornate goblet that belongs to old king Nestor. The inscription on the Pithecusan cup apparently alludes to that passage:

> I am Nestor's thirst-quenching cup.
> Longing for Aphrodite, beautifully crowned,
> shall immediately seize the drinker.[10]

The Pithecusan "Nestor's cup" is rich in historical significance. It is not only evidence of the spread of literacy through trade and colonization but it exemplifies the Greeks' love of pleasure and their tendency to identify with the legends of their heroic past, qualities that surely contributed to the dynamism of their culture.

Historical Background II: The Archaic Period

The earliest of the poets translated in this volume lived in the seventh century. The biographical details that are known are prefaced to the translations of each one's work. In general terms, Greek culture continued to spread via colonization, and the city-states flourished and evolved. Of the earliest poets, Archilochus and Semonides help colonize the Aegean in the mid-seventh century, while Tyrtaeus and Alcman reveal different aspects of the culture of Sparta, the most militarist of the city-states, in its formative years near the end of that century.

Emerging from the dark age, most city-states were controlled by cliques of ancestral nobles. In the past, kings had been chosen from these same families, but by this time oligarchies had replaced monarchies in most places. With increasing prosperity, many people gained wealth who were excluded because of birth from political office. This caused resentment and frequent revolutions by which one man, the champion of the disenfranchised, would gain absolute power. Such rulers were known as tyrants. This was not a term of abuse, originally, but the fact that tyrants had absolute power and *could* abuse it made tyranny a frightening prospect to many.

Shortly after 600, in order to avoid a tyranny, all factions in Athens agreed to authorize the patriot Solon to reform the laws in a way that would protect the nobles' wealth while giving others access to political power and helping the desperately poor. The main purpose of

Solon's surviving poetry is to defend his reforms, which set Athens on the road to democracy. Alcaeus and many of the poems attributed to Theognis deal with the same political problems but take the point of view of ancestral nobles. Despite Solon's reforms, Athens did fall under the sway of a tyranny, that of Pisistratus and his sons, which lasted from mid-century until the expulsion of Pisistratus' son Hippias in 510 B.C. At this point, however, the Athenians adopted further constitutional reforms, which mark the birth of democracy.

As mentioned above, Greek colonies on the Turkish coast did not initially confront any organized foreign powers, but inland kingdoms eventually developed under the influence of the Assyrians. The Phrygians were dominant in the eighth century but were overrun by barbarian nomads, the Cimmerians, around 700 and ceased to be influential. Afterwards, Lydia enjoyed its brief period of splendor. Its capital was at Sardis, only fifty miles from the coast. The founder of its last and greatest dynasty was Gyges, who gained control of Sardis around 680. The Lydians were highly regarded by the Greeks but were an occasional military threat. We catch glimpses of the military struggles of this period in the poetry of Callinus and Mimnermus.

Assyrian power crumbled near the end of the seventh century. Subject states rebelled successfully and divided the empire. The most powerful of the victors were the Medes, who ended up controlling the northern portion of the Assyrian realm from the north coast of the Persian Gulf to Cappadocia (central Turkey). West of Cappadocia lay Lydia. The Medes invaded it early in the sixth century, but were repulsed. Supposedly, the last battle ended in mutual panic when a full solar eclipse occurred, probably in 585. The former adversaries agreed to a treaty by which they became allies.

The Lydians prospered mightily for the next few decades. Their last king, Croesus, was famous for piety as well as for wealth. Though he compelled Greek city-states on the coast to pay him tribute, he sent gifts to the temples of Apollo at Delphi and Artemis at Ephesus.

Croesus' allies, the Medes, did not fare so well. The southeastern tip of their kingdom was inhabited by a kindred people, the Persians. Under the leadership of the famous Cyrus, the Persians rose up and conquered their masters. Croesus reacted to the Persian conquest of the Median empire by invading its westernmost extension, Cappadocia. The Persians repelled his attack and invaded Lydia. Sardis fell.

Soon thereafter the Greek city-states on the coast surrendered to the Persians. The lyric poets Phocylides, Hipponax, Xenophanes, and Anacreon lived in Ionia at the time of the Persian takeover; the latter two emigrated.

Croesus, whose actual fate is unknown, quickly became a legendary figure. A imaginative version of his career is one of the chief topics in the first book of Herodotus' history. Of the poets in this volume, Bacchylides tells us that Croesus was about to burn himself and his family on a funeral pyre when Sardis fell, but Apollo whisked them all away to Hyperborea.

Persian rule was more irksome to the Greeks than was Lydian rule. In 500, the Ionian states rebelled. The rebellion was quickly subdued, but not before the city of Athens sent aid to the rebels. In 490, the Persian emperor Darius tried to punish Athens. A Persian force landed at Marathon but was unexpectedly defeated by a smaller band of defenders. Ten years later, the next emperor, Xerxes, launched a massive land and sea invasion of Greece. The invasion was stalled by 300 Spartans, who fought to the death at Thermopylae. The Persian navy was defeated by the Greeks under the leadership of Athens at Salamis; on the ground, the Spartans led the Greeks to victory at the battle of Plataea. These victories made the Greeks a force to reckon with in the Aegean and eastern Mediterranean, and they mark the beginning of the Classical period. Of the poets in this volume, Simonides lived in Athens during the period of the Persian wars and may be the author of a famous epitaph for the Spartans who died at Thermopylae.

Greek culture in the "west," i.e., southern Italy and Sicily, evolved somewhat differently. Whereas tyrannies were superseded on mainland Greece and in the east by democracy, which spread rapidly from Athens, they continued to flourish in the west. Bacchylides and Pindar composed their best-known poems to honor Olympic victories won by tyrants of western Greek cities. Chronologically, both poets belong to the Classical period, since they reached maturity during the Persian Wars. The literature of the Classical period, however, was dominated by new genres that evolved in democratic Athens: tragedy, history, philosophy, and oratory. In genre and spirit, Bacchylides and Pindar are more strongly linked to the archaic past. Samples of their work give us a sense of what the complete songs of the earlier choral poets—Alcman, Stesichorus, Ibycus, and Simonides—were like.

Ancient Greek Meter and Types of Lyric Poetry

Ancient Greeks made no distinction between poetry and song. All poems had easily perceived rhythms; listeners could—and sometimes did—tap their feet or clap hands in time with the poet. Beyond that, it is difficult for a modern English-speaker to gain a clear notion of the sound of ancient Greek poetry. For one thing, Greek words did not have stress accents. Instead, Greeks were sensitive to the length of time it that it took to pronounce different kinds of syllables. Those that were "closed"—i.e., ended in two or more consonants—or contained a long vowel or diphthong were perceived as taking twice as long to pronounce as "open" syllables containing short vowels. A line of Greek poetry consisted of a certain number of poetic feet—set combinations of long and short syllables. Dactylic hexameter, for example, consisted of five dactyls (a dactyl being a long syllable followed by two short syllables) plus a spondee (two long syllables) with other spondees substituted at the poet's discretion for any or all of the dactyls. When a poetic line was read, the beat was perceived as falling on the syllables that were regularly long, e.g., on the first syllable in a dactyl or spondee in a dactylic line. In reading ancient Greek poetry, English-speakers naturally express the rhythm by stressing the syllables receiving the downbeat, but experts in Greek metrics maintain that such practice creates a false impression and that for the original audience the duration of syllables alone conveyed the rhythm.[11]

Another problem is that, though much Greek poetry was meant to be sung, only a few scraps of verse with musical notation have survived. Hence many ancient Greek poems are really songs to which we know the words and to some extent the rhythm, but not the tune.

The least musical of ancient Greek poems were "stichic" compositions (from *stichos*, line), i.e., poems consisting of one kind of metrical line repeated indefinitely. Besides dactylic hexameter, iambic trimeter and trochaic tetrameter were the most frequent kinds of stichic verse.[12] Stichic verse was apparently recited rhythmically with little, if any, musical intonation and no instrumental accompaniment.

Verses in which lines in two or three different meters alternated were somewhat more musical. Most common were elegiac couplets, each consisting of a dactylic hexameter followed by a shorter dactylic line. There is abundant evidence that they were sometimes sung to the accompaniment of wind instruments known as *double pipes* (pairs of fairly short reeds joined at the mouthpiece), but specialists disagree on whether that was the regular practice. Other poems in which a long metrical line is followed by one or two shorter ones are known as "epodes" (from *epi,* after, and *ode,* song). As with elegy, it is not really known what role music played in their performance. Modern classicists lump iambic and trochaic verse, elegies and epodes together as a basic subdivision of Greek poetry, i.e., less musical lyric poetry. Early lyric poets whose verse falls into this category are Archilochus, Semonides, Callinus, Mimnermus, Tyrtaeus, Solon, Phocylides, Hipponax, Xenophanes, and Theognis. As this list suggests, Ionians dominated the field of stichic, elegiac, and epodic verse.

Compositions in other meters, called "melic" by specialists (from *melos,* song), were sung, accompanied by pipes or lyre, either by solo performers or by choruses, who also danced. Melic compositions are characterized by great metrical variety and freedom. Solo songs are divided into short, metrically equivalent stanzas, and they were especially associated with the Aeolic poets, Sappho and Alcaeus. Choral songs establish a metrical pattern in an initial unit known as a *strophe* (turning), which usually consists of about ten lines of different rhythms and lengths. The pattern is repeated in the next unit, the *antistrophe* (reverse turn), then a different, shorter pattern is introduced in a unit called an "epode" or "after-song" in a second sense of the term. This triadic structure (AAB) is then repeated indefinitely. The Dorians—such as Alcman, Stesichorus, and Ibycus—were the earliest masters of choral song. In late Archaic and early Classical times, ethnic divisions blurred. The Ionian Anacreon wrote solo songs; the Ionians Simonides and Bacchylides and the Aeolic Pindar wrote choral songs.

We have a broad idea of the occasions on which lyric poems were performed. The worship of the Olympian gods pervaded Greek life. Music contests as well as athletic competitions were regularly held in temple precincts to honor the resident deity. Some choral poems, e.g., Alcman's *partheneia* (songs to be sung by maidens [*parthenoi*]), were composed for such events. Victory odes were not performed competitively themselves, but they were often integrated into religious observances in temple precincts either at the site of the victory or in the victor's homeland. Otherwise they were performed at specially grand banquets in the victor's honor.

Solo songs, on the other hand, were a regular feature of banquets. Greek vases with painted pictures give us a vivid impression of this institution. Diners lay on couches with their heads wreathed. They drank from painted cups and were supported by embroidered cushions, and as they drank, they sang. Sometimes they were accompanied by a young servant playing pipes; sometimes they accompanied themselves on the lyre.

In the early days, at least, music seems to have been in the hands of the amateurs. We really have no idea of what "being a poet" meant in practical terms to an Archilochus or a Sappho. By the beginning of the Classical period, however, leading poets were well paid by tyrants and aristocrats to provide them with the best of victory songs, poetic inscriptions, and other compositions. Both Anacreon and Pindar spoke nostalgically of the days before poetry had "a silver sheen," i.e., before poets composed for money (Anacreon 32).

My translations are in free verse. I have, however, reproduced the shape of the Greek originals, keeping the number of lines, their relative lengths, and stanza divisions the same. Regarding syntax and diction, the poets represented in this volume composed for the generality of the educated public; there were no professional literary critics to impress. Language is traditional and moderately elevated. Except in the case of Pindar, there is little ostentatious verbal ingenuity; meaning is almost always crystal clear. I have tried diligently to preserve these qualities in translation.

Some Main Themes of Early Greek Poetry

Part of the appeal of Homer, Hesiod, and the lyric poets in this volume is that they deal in a searching manner with universal questions and problems. Near the end of the *Iliad*, for example, Homer's Achilles presents a grimly fatalistic view of life to the Trojan king, Priam. The random "gifts" of the gods are responsible for joy and suffering, and the latter predominates (24.527–33):

There stands by Zeus' door a pair of jars
containing the evils he gives; another has blessings.
When a man receives a mixture from Zeus the thunderer,
he encounters good and bad by turns in his life,
but when Zeus' gifts are mean, a man is despised;
wretched hunger drives him across the earth,
he wanders deprived of honor by gods and men.

Zeus himself expresses a different opinion in the *Odyssey's* first speech. Citing the case of Aegisthus, Agamemnon's murderer, he argues that human beings are responsible for their own worst sufferings (1.32–33):

How mortals lay the blame on gods! *Popoi!*
They say their evils come from us, but their own
foolishness causes them pain beyond what is fated.

Hesiod also expresses the view that Zeus is just and that human suffering results from greed and laziness. It would not be correct to say that either opinion particularly characterized the ancient Greeks. Rather, they were interested in the question of whether individuals are principally responsible for their own happiness, and their literature contains, in effect, an ongoing debate on this issue among many others.

The fragments of the lyric poets are somewhat confusing at first reading. Many of the poems were brief and personal to begin with, and now only portions of them survive. One way to approach them is to note how they participate in the grand debates initiated as far as we can tell by Homer and Hesiod. For example, grimly fatalistic views of life similar to Achilles' are found in the following fragments: Archilochus 30, 32; Semonides 1, 3; Mimnermus 5; Simonides 17, 24, 25, 31, 32. Solon, on the other hand, warns the Athenians not to blame the gods for problems that they bring upon themselves (8, 24). That point of view is countered in turn by the assertion that the very ability to be virtuous depends on fate and the gifts of the gods, a thought that is expressed concisely by Archilochus (26) and lies behind Simonides' philosophy of toleration (5–13).

The dependence of human happiness on the caprice of fortune is contrasted in several powerful passages with the universal human tendency towards blind optimism (Semonides 3; Solon 25.33–42;

Simonides 32, 33). We are urged to overcome wishful thinking and, in contemporary terms, internalize the fact that bad things can and will happen to us. There is, however, something to be said for positive thinking. Theognis seems to acknowledge this in saying that Hope is the only divinity left on earth (1135–46). Bacchylides' Apollo tries to strike a balance by saying that we should have two firm convictions: that we are going to die tomorrow, and that we are going to live and prosper for another fifty years (5.76–83).

Another important theme is old age, which is often mentioned as the worst of the gods' "gifts." In the *Iliad*, King Priam symbolizes the pathos of aging, but vigorous old Nestor is a counterexample. Lyric poets who lament growing old stress its negative impact on one's love life: see Mimnermus 4, 5, 6, 7, 8; Alcman 3; Anacreon 23; Theognis 527. Others, however, deal with aging in an upbeat way (Solon 9; Simonides 21; Xenophanes 15). Bacchylides' third victory ode was written to console an elderly, ailing tyrant: one's body may fail, but virtues still shine bright.

Warfare, a constant feature of ancient Greek life, is a central concern of Homer and most of the lyric poets. The question of whether soldiers should risk their lives in battle inevitably arises. The consensus among Homer's heroes is eloquently expressed by the Lycian hero Sarpedon: an early death is a fair price for immortal glory (*Iliad* 12.322–28), but in the *Odyssey*, Achilles' ghost rejects the idea (*Odyssey* 11.488–91). The lyric poets frequently adapt Sarpedon's sentiments to their own circumstances (Callinus, Mimnermus 2, Tyrtaeus, Solon 20 and 21, and Simonides 15 and 20). Archilochus is the only one who specifically rejects the notion of death before dishonor (12, 33).

Then as now athletics provided an opportunity for glorious conflict that was less destructive than war, and successful athletes were idolized. The funeral games for Patroclus in *Iliad* 23 and the victory odes of Bacchylides and Pindar attest to athletes' central place in Greek society, but even here the opposition is heard from. Tyrtaeus (9) says that athletes deserve no praise compared to warriors, and Xenophanes (3) asserts that his wisdom is more valuable than athletic prowess.

Although his stories are set in a male chauvinist world, Homer's depiction of relationships between the sexes is evenhanded. As the case of Helen shows, women as well as men sometimes have their judgment overwhelmed by sexual desire. Men, however, are more vulnerable, and some women use this fact to manipulate them, e.g., Hera with Zeus and Penelope with her suitors. As for the men, when the fever passes, their attitude towards women changes into hostility proportionate to their earlier "love." During his reconciliation with Agamemnon, Achilles wishes that his slave girl Briseis had died before she caused so much trouble (*Iliad* 19.59–60).

The lyric poets describe sexual desire of all types, male and female, heterosexual and homosexual: see Archilochus 15, 28, 29; Alcman 1, 2, 10; Sappho 16, 20, 23; Ibycus 4, 5; Anacreon 4, 7, 12, 21, 26; Theognis 1259, 1299, 1345. Passion is usually experienced as disconcerting, if not downright painful, which helps explain why sexual desire is tinged with hostility, as is so evident in Archilochus' first fragment. Other examples of predatory male lust are provided by Hipponax 4 and Anacreon 1. Fragments in which male poets disparage women may also be seen as a reaction against the painful longings that they stir. The longest of these is Semonides 2, a derogatory catalog of female personalities based on animals; Phocylides 6 and Hipponax 7 are similar in spirit.

Sappho's poems provide a feminine foil for these masculine attitudes. In two fragments (10, 11) she laments the loss of female virginity. Elsewhere she introduces a feminine perspective into Homer's world. She describes the arrival of Andromache as a newly-wed in Troy (4). She cites Helen's life as proof of the supremacy of love in human affairs (5). She asks Aphrodite to join her in battle, to help her win the heart of her latest lover (8). Though composed by a man, Alcman's *partheneia* also present a very feminine point of view.

The *Iliad* depicts warriors whose behavior is brutally direct. Achilles is typical. "As hateful to me as the gates of death," he says, "is the man who hides one thing in his heart and says something else (9.312–13)." The *Odyssey*, however, is set in a more civilized society where hypocrisy is the rule, and a major theme in this epic and in the lyric poets is that people are rarely what they seem (Archilochus 4; Alcaeus 7; Phocylides 2, 4; Theognis 53, 83.) The usual reaction to the fact that we live in a a dishonest world is to practice preemptive duplicity, as in Theognis 213–18. Again Solon is an exception: people who assumed that he did not mean what he said were grievously surprised (5).

The Preservation of the Lyric Poems

Throughout the Archaic and Classical periods, people learned litera-
ture through oral performance, and that was especially true of lyric
poetry. Individuals did have copies made for themselves of their
favorite works. There is, however, no evidence at first of an organ-
ized book trade or of public libraries. The first Greeks known to have
had large private collections of texts were Euripides and Aristotle.

The first two public libraries were established in Alexandria by the
Ptolemaic kings of Egypt at the beginning of the Hellenistic period,
i.e., early in the third century B.C. Another great library was
founded in Pergamum a century later. Private collections became
increasingly common as well. Scholars in Alexandria and Pergamum
worked on learned editions of Classical works. Most ancient Greek
literature is preserved today on medieval and Renaissance manu-
scripts, which are copies of copies etc., deriving ultimately from the
work of Hellenistic scholars. Of all the poems in this volume, how-
ever, only Pindar's and the Theognidean anthology survive in that
way.

At the heart of this collection are 288 fragments that represent the
most significant remains of the early lyric poets from Archilochus to
Simonides. Of these, thirty are preserved on the remains of ancient
scrolls made out of papyrus. Nearly all surviving "papyri" come from
the dry sands of Egypt. This country was Hellenized as a result of
Alexander's conquest, and many of its inhabitants collected literary
works. The literary fragments that have been recovered in modern
times are the remnants of scrolls once housed in the private libraries
of Hellenized Egyptians or transplanted Greeks. Most such frag-
ments are dated to the first or second century A.D. The existence of
ancient papyri was known for some time, but it did not excite much
interest until the spectacular finds of Sir Wallis Budge, a British Egyp-
tologist, who collected antiquities for the British Museum in the Near
East in the late nineteenth century. In Egypt he collaborated with
private Egyptian dealers in defiance of the government. In 1889, he
acquired papyri from Roman-period tombs near Malawi, which had
been secretly excavated at his suggestion by Egyptian associates. One
of these tombs turned out to contain an important lost work by Aris-
totle or one of his students, the *Constitution of the Athenians*. The

papyrus containing most of Bacchylides' extant work was found in the same tombs by an independent operator. Budge purchased it after long negotiation and smuggled it out of Egypt with great difficulty because of the interest stirred by the Aristotle papyrus. While Budge diverted customs officials by refusing to let them open a crate of oranges, an Egyptian friend carried the Bacchylides papyrus past the checkpoint inside a gift-wrapped box.[13]

Most other papyrus texts come from ancient Oxyrhynchus (modern El Bahnasa). Nearly deserted now, in antiquity Oxyrhynchus was a bustling city with a theater designed to hold eleven thousand spectators. For centuries, papyrus scrolls were discarded in a rubbish heap on the outskirts of the city. Between 1896 and 1907, Oxford scholars Grenfell and Hunt excavated the site with the permission of the Egyptian government. Publication of the huge cache of papyri that they found continues to the present; volume 51 of *Oxyrhynchus Papyri* appeared in 1988.

Other papyri have been found in a variety of ways and have come into smaller collections throughout the world. They are usually cited by the city in which they are preserved and by a catalog number. The Louvre Papyrus (Alcman 2) was discovered by the great French Egyptologist, Auguste Mariette, in 1855. Mummy wrappings were often made out of discarded papyrus scrolls. Cologne 58 (Archilochus 1–2) was first published in 1974 after being recovered from the wrappings of a mummy housed in Austria; the Lille papyrus (Stesichorus 1), published in 1977, came from a French mummy.

The remaining fragments in this book are quotations found in the works of later, ancient authors. Four such authors account for over half of the fragments in this selection: Plutarch, Hephaestion, Athenaeus, and Stobaeus.

Plutarch was born about A.D. 46 and lived until at least 120. A native of Chaeronea in Boeotia and the son of a philosopher, he was a pious man who was a priest of Apollo at Delphi throughout the latter part of his life. A voluminous writer, he is best known for a collection of biographies, *Parallel Lives of Greeks and Romans,* which is an extremely important source for historians. He also wrote some seventy extant essays known collectively as the *Moralia.* As the name implies, they are mostly exhortations to virtue. Plutarch's writings preserve Archilochus 7–13, Tyrtaeus 4, Solon 10–17, Stesichorus 4, Ibycus 2, and Simonides 17–20.

Among authors whose works survive, **Hephaestion** is antiquity's foremost expert on poetic meters. He may have been the same Hephaestion who is mentioned as a tutor of the emperor Verus, Marcus Aurelius' brother, who was born in A.D. 130. He wrote a treatise on meters in forty-eight volumes, which was abridged to the surviving one-volume *Handbook on Meters*. Manuscripts transmit this work with two appendices on the structures of entire poems (called *Concerning a Poem* and *Concerning Poems*) and a third on punctuation (*Concerning Signs*). Because of its dense, technical language the text is comprehensible only to specialists, but it is a rich source of brief quotations from the lyric poets. For example, this is chapter 7 (sections 7–8) of the *Handbook*:

Acatalectic dactylic pentameter is called the Sapphic 14-syllable; Sappho's whole second book was written in it:

Once I loved you Atthis, long ago.

Acatalectic dactylic tetrameter is like this:

Eros leaves me limp and reeling,
that bittersweet, implacable serpent.
Atthis, you hated the very thought of me.
And now you fly to Andromeda!

There are also so-called logaoedic dactyls, which have dactyls elsewhere but a trochaic syzygy in the last place. Most noteworthy of these is that which has atrochaic syzygy after two dactyls and is called the Alcaic ten-syllable:

And you dwell on the borders;

and that which has the syzygy after three dactyls and is called the Praxilleion:

O woman prettily glancing through the doors,
maiden in the face but wife below.[14]

Hephaestion is the source of Archilochus 15, Alcman 6, Sappho 17–29, Hipponax 4, Anacreon 4–12, and Simonides 22.

Athenaeus flourished around A.D. 200. He was a native of Naucra-

tis, an ancient Greek emporium on the Nile, and one of the great
pedants of all time. His sole surviving work, *Deipnosophistae* (*Sophists'
Banquet* or more literally *Dinner-Sophists*) originally contained thirty
volumes; fifteen survive. They are in the form of a wide-ranging
conversation carried on by a large cast of characters, leading intellec-
tuals of the day. The dialogue form, however, is overwhelmed by the
huge number of quotations that are inserted into it. Whenever a word
or topic captures a speaker's attention, he recites every known occur-
rence of it in the classics. The result is a disorganized, wildly uneven
book of quotations. It is the source of Archilochus 17–24, Mimnermus
1, Alcman 7–11, Alcaeus 10–17, Sappho 30–31, Stesichorus 5–6,
Ibycus 3–4, Hipponax 5–6, Xenophanes 2–5, Anacreon 14–22, and
Simonides 26.

Our most important source is **Stobaeus,** who lived in the fifth
century A.D. and compiled a four-volume anthology of quotations
from Classical literature. Excerpts include prose and poetry and are
arranged by subject matter under different rubrics, e.g., Archilochus
25 ("I lie racked by desire," etc.) is in a chapter entitled, "Concerning
The Vulgar Aphrodite Who Is The Reason For Procreation And About
Desire For The Pleasures Of The Flesh"; Hipponax 7 ("A woman
pleases twice," etc.) comes under the rubric "That Marrying Is Not
Good," which is preceded by quotations implying "That Marriage Is
Most Fair." Other topics range from metaphysics to household man-
agement. Unlike Athenaeus' selections, all of Stobaeus' are meaning-
ful; some, like Semonides' catalog of women, are quite long. He is
the source of Archilochus 26–33, Semonides 1–5, Callinus 1, Mimner-
mus 2–8, Tyrtaeus 8–9, Solon 25–26, Sappho 40–41, Phocylides 4–7,
Hipponax 7, Xenophanes 16, Anacreon 23, and Simonides 29–34.

Other fragments are thinly spread over thirty-five different
authors and a handful of anonymous sources, such as "scholia" or
marginal notes on manuscripts. The authors range in time from Hero-
dotus in the fifth century B.C. to John Tzetzes, who lived in Con-
stantinople in the twelfth century of our era. Essential information
about all of these sources is given in an appendix at the end of this
volume.

I have given more than the usual prominence below to the manner
in which each fragment has been transmitted, putting ancient papy-
rus texts first, followed by literary excerpts in chronological order. I
have renumbered fragments in accordance with this scheme. My

number for each fragment appears in brackets at its end. A concordance of these numbers with those in standard editions is given in a separate appendix. Except for quotations from Hephaestion and Stobaeus, I have given summaries of the broad context in which the excerpt is lodged and often the exact words by which it is introduced. As indicated above, Stobaeus does not discuss his excerpts at all and Hephaestion's analysis only concerns the metrical qualities of the Greek. In other cases, knowing contexts can add to our appreciation of the fragments. We could not be sure that Archilochus 5 and Alcaeus 8 and 9 were allegorical without Heraclitus' accompanying remarks. Two of Sappho's best odes (fragments 8 and 16) are embedded in outstanding examples of ancient literary criticism. The evidence that Simonides composed the most famous of ancient epitaphs (fragment 1: "Tell them in Sparta," etc.) consists of the ambiguous context in which Herodotus transmits it. Equally important, the context of a literary citation tells us just what we really know about the original poem and prevents false assumptions in that regard. Quoting out of context is always misleading, and doubly so when one quotes a quotation.

Translations

Archilochus of Paros

(7th cent. B.C.)

Archilochus is a major artist and an intriguing historical puzzle. Composing about 650, he was a native of the island of Paros, one of the Cyclades that was settled by the Mycenaean Greeks. His father was the leader of a Parian colony on the northern Aegean island of Thasos, four miles from the Thracian shore. In antiquity, gold was mined on Thasos. Before the settlers from Paros came, it was occupied by Thracians and Phoenician traders. The Parians built a city there and several outposts on the Thracian shore, but not without a struggle. They clashed with the Thracians and their own neighbors from the island of Naxos, who also wanted to colonize the area. Archilochus took part in these struggles, and they were a major topic in his poetry. He presents himself as a warrior poet (23) with an irreverent attitude, boasting of losing his shield to a Thracian to save his life (12), ridiculing pretentious military commanders (6, 14), boastful comrades (9), and Thasos' appearance (8).

Claudius Aelianus (1st/2nd cent. A.D.) preserves a passage in which Plato's uncle Critias (no saint himself) lists unflattering elements in Archilochus' self-portrait. If it were not for his own poetry, he writes,

> we would not know that he was the son of a slave named *Enipe* [Insult], that he left Paros for Thasos because of desperate poverty, that he became the enemy of the people there, or that he slandered friends and foes alike. In addition, we would not be aware that he was an adulterer, if we did not learn it from him, nor that he was licentious and violent, and worse that he discarded his shield. (*Miscellaneous Stories* 10.13)

Despite or because of all this, Archilochus became a legendary hero on Paros and a shrine was erected in his memory. Two long inscriptions recording his supposed achievements have been found

on it. After narrating the establishment of the shrine, which was
commanded by Apollo's oracle, the earlier inscription by one Mne-
siepes (ca. 250 B.C.) describes a miraculous meeting between the
young Archilochus and the Muses; the establishment of a Dionysiac
rite on Paros at Archilochus' urging; and verses in which Archilochus
rallied the men of Paros to victory over Naxos in a fierce war. This
third portion originally contained a thirty-line quotation; unfortu-
nately only the first dozen or so letters of each line survive: "They fill
with smoke . . . / in ships, but the rapid . . . / of enemies, it was
dried . . ." etc.

The later inscription by a certain Sosthenes (ca. 100 B.C.) says that
the miraculous salvation by a dolphin of a shipwrecked Milesian was
commemorated in one of Archilochus' poems, and it gives a muti-
lated account (including quotations from Archilochus) of another bat-
tle against the Naxians. A seventh-century cenotaph honoring Glau-
cus, son of Leptines, whom Archilochus addresses as a friend in
several fragments, was found on Thasos in 1951. In 1961, a fourth-
century inscription marking Archilochus' own burial was found on
Paros.

Despite all this evidence, it is difficult to draw a picture of Archi-
lochus' life. It is a truism of modern scholarship that even when they
are cast in the first person, poems and songs are not reliable sources
of biographical inference, since poets and songwriters freely adopt
fictitious identities. Ancient scholars, however, assumed that first-
person poetry was a straightforward reflection of experience and
wrote "biographies" of poets based on this premise. Critias' infer-
ences about Archilochus exemplify this principle in operation, as do
the stories in Mnesiepes' inscription. Ancient biographical state-
ments that seem to derive from poetry are generally dismissed by
modern scholars.

Archilochus wrote about love as well as war, and his treatment of
that theme gave rise to another biographical tradition in antiquity.
Supposedly, he was engaged to a certain Neobule, but her father,
Lycambes, prevented the match. Thereafter Archilochus ridiculed the
whole family so fiercely that they all committed suicide. A similar
story was told of the targets of Hipponax' abuse. Neither should be
believed.

What we do know about the author then is that he gained fame
by composing songs in which he adopted a rascally persona to com-

ment on the Parian settlement of Thasos and other matters. As with
any contemporary singer, we do not know whether his first-person
statements were based on experience, imagination, or both, but the
archaeological evidence suggests that he and his friends were among
the leaders of Parian society. Therefore his accounts of disreputable
adventures and sentiments were probably designed to be understood
as fictional. But we are still left with the impression that the society
that embraced such a singer as a hero must have been rather broad-
minded.

Papyrus Fragments

A Cologne papyrus (2nd cent. A.D.), recovered from a mummy, pre-
serves the description of an erotic encounter between a poet and a
girl. The reference to Neobule and the fact that the next poem on the
papyrus is definitely by Archilochus incline most experts to assign
this poem to him as well. When the fragment becomes intelligible,
the girl is speaking, trying to fend off Archilochus' advances.

"If lust for the acts you urge brooks
no delay,
there lives with us a lovely,

gentle maid who longs to marry.
Her form is perfection.
Make her your own dear wife."

I answered her speech, point by point.
"Child of a fine
lady, Amphimedo, imprisoned

now in the damp earth, for young
men the goddess
provides numerous pleasures

besides the divine thing. Any
will do, and we
shall consider the question at leisure

tonight, you, the goddess, and I,
the decision being yours,
but I have a pressing need.

Just concede the lower walls
and area around
the gate. My advance will stop

in the grassy garden. Neobule? *Aiai!*
Some other man
can have her. Her fruit is overripe.

Maidenhood's flower has gone to seed.
Her charm is withered.
⌈Never satisfied in youth,

⌊she is now a woman governed by passion.
The crows can have her!
Zeus, never decree

that I become a local laughingstock
by having such
a wife. I far prefer

a simple, honest girl like you.
Neobule is fast;
she has a legion of lovers.

I fear I would bear 'blind puppies
and miscarriages,' if I did
anything rash with her."

Finished with talk, I grabbed the girl
and laid her down
on a bed of flowers. My cloak

provided shelter. I held her neck
in the crook of my arm.
She was frozen with fear, like a fawn.

With my hands I fondled her breasts, whose smoothness
evinced puberty's
recent arrival, and the rest

of her beautiful body, then shot my white
force, lightly
touching her yellow hair.[1] [1]

The same papyrus scrap contains the beginning of a second poem.
The first two lines are quoted by Hephaestion as belonging to Archi-
lochus:

The bloom is off your delicate skin; it is cracked
     and furrowed. The ills of old age
are taking over. Sweet desire has fled
     your once desired face. The blasts
of many a storm have ravaged you. [2]

An Oxyrhynchus papyrus (2nd cent. A.D.) contains the description of a conversation between a poet and a woman, who seem to be partners in an underhanded scheme. Attribution to Archilochus is based on a frequently quoted saying of his among the mutilated lines that follow: "Different men cheer their hearts in different ways."

> I replied,
> "Lady, have no fear of bad things
> people say. I will take care of
> tonight. Just grant me good will.
> Could you really think I sank to such
> a depth? Perhaps I looked lowborn.
> But that is not my nature or my family's.
> I know how to be a friend to my friend
> and how to hate enemies and hurt them,
> like an ant; there is truth in that saying.
> . . . Regard this city,
> which men have never plundered; but you
> have taken it by sword, gaining glory.
> Be its lord! Hold the power!
> Many the men who will envy you!" [3]

Quotations

In *Eudemian Ethics*, Aristotle (4th cent. B.C.) lists different kinds of friendship. He says that the most frequent kind is based on utility.

> People like each other because they are useful to each other and only so long as they are, as in the proverb:
>
> > Glaucus, a comrade in arms is a friend forever—
> > until the battle ends." [4]

Scholars attribute the lines to Archilochus because of their being addressed to a Glaucus; see fragments 5 and 16.

Heraclitus (1st cent. A.D.), a literary scholar, begins an essay on Homer's allegories with a general definition of allegory as meaning one thing while saying (*agoreuein*) others (*alla*).

> For example, when Archilochus is caught up in his terrible hardships in Thrace he compares the war to a stormy sea, saying:

> Look at the breakers, Glaucus, rising far out,
> and clouds pile up beside the peaks of Gyrae,
> the sign of storm. Fears come true when least expected. [5]

Dio Chrysostom (1st/2nd cent. A.D.) traveled the Roman empire giving morally edifying speeches. Speaking to the people of Tarsus, he tells them that their city's spiritual qualities are more important than its material advantages, which are considerable. By the same token, he says,

> Archilochus, Apollo's favorite, says this regarding a military commander:
>
> > I hate a tall commander, one who swaggers,
> > combs his wavy hair and trims his beard.
>
> Instead, he says,
>
> > give me one with crooked legs, who stands
> > firmly and has hairy shins. [6]

See fragment 14 for a slightly different version of these lines.

Plutarch is the source of the next seven fragments. The first comes from an essay concerning a mysterious inscription at Delphi. It consisted of the letter epsilon, pronounced *ei*. One theory was that the letter alluded to the many wishes addressed to Apollo. As Plutarch explains,

> People making wishes begin them with the words *ei gar* [if only]; for example, Archilochus says:
>
> > If only I could lay a hand on Neobule! [7]

Fragment 35 may be the continuation of this wish.

Writing on the topic of exile, Plutarch asserts that it has advantages, such as freedom from responsibility, but people disregard them:

> We are like Archilochus who overlooked the wheat fields and vineyards of Thasos and disparaged the island because of its rough terrain and irregular shape, saying:

This island is like an ass' back,
full of slopes and bristling. [8]

Describing the assassination of the emperor Galba in A.D. 69 at Otho's instigation, Plutarch says that afterwards everyone was anxious to ingratiate himself with Otho by claiming involvement.

As Archilochus says,

Seven were the enemies we overtook and slew; a thousand,
the comrades who claimed to have killed one. [9]

So too then many people not involved in the murder bloodied their hands and swords, displayed them, and claimed a reward.

On the topic of how to study poetry, Plutarch says that well-educated youths will derive beneficial lessons even from poems that might be suspected of being base:

Archilochus cannot be commended when, saddened by the death of his brother-in-law at sea, he decided to combat sorrow with drinking and sport and uttered these reprehensible words:

Crying is no cure; pursuing pleasure and feasting
does no one any harm. [10]

In reading this, according to Plutarch, we should reflect that wholesome activities in a time of grief do even less harm than self-indulgence.

Plutarch quotes the next fragment, without naming the author, to make the point that we should think about those less fortunate than ourselves, not those who are more fortunate. The first line is also quoted by Aristotle and attributed to Archilochus.[2]

Golden Gyges means nothing to me,
who was never snagged by envy. I do not
resent what the gods have done or long
for empire; it lies beyond my gaze. [11]

In an essay on the Spartans, Plutarch claims that Archilochus once visited their city, but the Spartans exiled him within an hour of learning that he had written that it was better to lose one's shield than to die:

Some Thracian is waving the shield I reluctantly left
    by a bush, a flawless piece.
So what? I saved myself. Forget the shield.
    I will get another, no worse. [12]

In his life of Theseus, Plutarch asserts that Theseus shaved his head in the front to avoid giving enemies anything to grab. In doing this, he was imitating the Abantes, a Euboean tribe mentioned by Homer:

These were warlike men, spear-fighters and masters at breaking through the enemy's ranks, as Archilochus bears witness in these lines:

Not many bows will bend or slings whirl,
    when Ares' collision shakes
the plain, but swords will have painful employment;
    for the masters of hand-to-hand combat
are there, the spear-famous lords of Euboea. [13]

The physician Galen (2nd cent. A.D.) invokes Archilochus' authority when discussing human limbs. His recollection of these lines differs from that of Dio Chrysostom (fragment 6).

Those called crooked or bandy-legged stand more firmly and are harder to turn back than those with straight limbs. This is made clear from the lines in which Archilochus says:

I hate a tall commander, one who swaggers.
Give me a small man with crooked legs,
who plants his feet firmly and is full of heart. [14]

From Hephaestion's *Handbook:*

But my friend, I succumb to the longing
    that loosens the limbs. [15]

The Christian writer Theophilus of Antioch (2nd cent. A.D.) quotes Archilochus to show that even pagans believe in punishing evil:

My one great talent lies in making
those who wrong me suffer horribly.[3] [16]

Athenaeus is the source of the next nine fragments. The first comes
from a discussion of wines mentioned by poets:

Archilochus compares Naxian wine to nectar and says somewhere:

I owe my bread to my spear and this Ismaric wine,
which I drink leaning on my spear. [17]

In a discussion of fruits, we learn that

excellent figs grow on the island of Paros. The Parians call them "bloody
figs," but they are the same as "Lydian figs." They get their name from
their red appearance. Archilochus refers to them when he says:

So long to Paros, those figs, and life by the sea. [18]

On the topic of marine life, Archilochus' authority is invoked for
the correct spelling of the accusative plural of "eel." The original
context must have been sexual:

You let a lot of blind eels in. [19]

In a discussion of drunkenness the point is made that thirst is the
strongest human desire.

Therefore Archilochus says:

Fighting you is water, and I
am thirsty. [20]

Aristotle is quoted as saying that under the influence of other
intoxicants people fall down in all directions but those overcome by
barley drinks or *pinon* (beer) only fall on their backs. Beer, we are told,
is called *bryton* by some authorities, as in the following lines by Archi-
lochus:

She toiled like a hunchback of Thrace
or Phrygia sucking beer through a straw. [21]

Athenaeus goes on to catalog the names for drinking cups found in poetry.

Archilochus uses the word *kothon* [tankard] of a drinking cup in his elegiac verse in these words:

> Be sure the tankard stops at every seaman's
>   bench. Open the vats.
> Leave only dregs behind. On a watch like this,
>   sobriety is not even possible. [22]

Later we are told that men used to consider courage and patriotism more glorious than fame as a poet. For example,

although he was a good poet, Archilochus boasted first of his involvement in his city's affairs and only then mentioned his poetic skills, saying:

> I serve the Lord of Battle and the Muses too;
>   for I recognize the beauty of their gift. [23]

Finally, Athenaeus mentions that in the past all the guests at feasts, not just entertainers, participated in singing—which helped maintain a dignified atmosphere.

For example, Archilochus says:

> I know how to lead the lovely dithyrambic song
> of King Dionysus, when my wits are blasted by wine. [24]

In his dictionary Orion of Thebes (5th cent. A.D.) uses a couplet from Archilochus to illustrate the use of the word *epirrhesis* (slander).

> No one who worries about slander, Aesimides,
>   has very many pleasures. [25]

Stobaeus' anthology is the source of the next eight fragments.

> Glaucus, son of Leptines, quality of character
> depends on the kind of day that Zeus provides. [26]

> Heart, reeling with sorrows, unsure what
> to do, stand and fight! Charge the hostile

line headfirst. Be steady in ambush as enemies
approach. Make no display of joy when you win;
losing, do not collapse in tears at home.
Enjoy the good times, regret the bad
in moderation. Learn about life's changing rhythm. [27]

Coiled by my heart, love's longing
misted my eyes and made off
with my fragile wits. [28]

I lie racked by desire,
lifeless. By will of the gods, cruel pains
penetrate my bones. [29]

All things are easy for gods. Often they put
men back on their feet, who crawled in dirt,
and often trip the successful in mid-stride, laying
them flat. Then evils swarm. A man becomes
a wanderer, lacking necessities, out of his mind. [30]

Call nothing unexpected or amazing or swear
it will not happen, for Zeus, Olympian father,
hid the sun's bright light, making
night from noon, and clammy fear descended
on men. Now everything is credible. Nothing turns
heads. No one should even blink if he sees
dolphins trade their underwater homes to lions,
and the ocean's crashing waves are suddenly dearer
than land to beasts who preferred the wooded hill.[4] [31]

No townsman in his cups will scoff at our painful loss,
    Pericles, nor will the city.
Such were the men the roaring sea has drowned,
    and we weep until our lungs
are swollen. But friend, the gods gave us endurance
    to medicate incurable evils.
They pass from man to man. They attack us now;
    we gape at the bleeding wound.
Soon others will feel it. Put feminine
    sorrow aside. Endure. [32]

No one in the city honors the dead or even
mentions them. Alive we prefer to court the living.
Nothing good can be said for being dead. [33]

A dictionary compiled about A.D. 1100 uses a crude line from Archilochus to illustrate the meaning of the root *tryge* (grain):

He had a cock like a grain-fed donkey stud. [34]

To cure the sterility of King Aegeus, Euripides' Medea advises him not to loosen the foot of his wineskin (*askon*) until he gets home. A scholiast comments that this means abstaining from sexual intercourse, since

here *askon* denotes the lower body around the stomach. Archilochus writes:

fall on her wineskin forcefully, pressing belly
to belly, thigh to thigh. [35]

These may have been the lines following fragment 4 in which Archilochus wishes to touch Neobule.

A scholiast commenting on the influential essay on rhetoric by Hermogenes (2nd cent. A.D.) uses lines from Archilochus to exemplify his mistaken notion that an "epode is always four syllables shorter than the previous line." The reference to Lycambes, traditionally the name of Neobule's father, is the basis of the attribution to Archilochus.

Father Lycambes, what have you said?
    Who knocked your brain loose?
Once mentally fit, you have now become
    the townsmen's biggest laugh. [36]

Semonides of Amorgos

(7th cent. B.C.)

The poet whom we call Semonides may be considered a poor man's Archilochus. He was a seventh-century native of Samos, one of the original Ionian colonies. He is credited by the *Suda*, a Byzantine encyclopedia, with establishing a Samian colony on the island of Amorgos, in the southeastern Aegean. Hence, like Archilochus, he was colonist and poet, and his attitudes are somewhat similar. Lucian lists him, Archilochus, and Hipponax as the masters of abusive verse. Semonides is most frequently remembered today for his long, jaundiced catalog of female personality types (see fragment 2).

There is some confusion about this author's name. In fact, he is called Simonides by all ancient sources except for a late grammarian who is quoted in a Byzantine encyclopedia, the *Etymologicum Magnum*, to the effect that the iambic poet from Amorgos was named Semonides, while the lyric poet of Ceos was named Simonides. This distinction has been kept by modern classicists merely for convenience. The significant fragments of "Semonides" all come from Stobaeus, who refers to their author as Simonides. Attribution of these fragments to the poet of Amorgos is based on the fact that they are written in iambic meter. Poems in other meters are attributed to Simonides of Ceos.

How easily the gods trick the mortal mind! [1]

    In the beginning, god made women
differently: one from the shaggy sow.
Everything lies in a jumble at home,
caked with mud and kicked in the dirt.
She sits unbathed in unclean rags   5
on heaps of dung, getting fatter.
    From the wicked fox he made another,
a woman capable of anything; not one

35

virtue or vice has gotten past her,
though often she damns the former and praises   10
the latter. Her character constantly changes.
    One from the dog, bad as her mother;
she has to see and hear it all.
She sniffs all around, then runs away
and barks, even if no one is there.   15
No threats from a husband can stop her noise,
not even bashing her teeth with a stone
suffices, much less gentle persuasion.
She acts the same, sitting with guests,
constantly yapping away unstoppable.   20
    The Olympians molded another woman
of earth and gave her lame to man,
knowing nothing evil or good.
The only job she understands is eating.
She cannot even move her chair   25
close to the fire in winter storms.[1]
    One from the sea with a twofold mind.
Sometimes she laughs and acts merry,
winning praise from the house guest:
"In all mankind, no woman excels   30
this wife of yours, and none is prettier."
Next day, she cannot endure being seen
or anyone near her; she rages, hard
to approach as a bitch protecting puppies,
impossible to please, cross with all,   35
treating friend and foe alike.
As the sea often lies calm,
harmless, a great joy to sailors
in the summer season, but often rages,
tossing about in thunderous waves;   40
this woman's character most resembles
the sea, whose temperament is always changing.
    One from the sullen, gray mule.
With force and threats she finally learns
to like her work and do it well   45
enough. Meanwhile, she eats all night
and all day in a nook or by the hearth.
Likewise, she welcomes any companion
who comes to her for the work of Aphrodite.
    The weasel woman is a wretched, pitiable   50
breed without a single attractive,
desirable, pleasant, or lovable trait.
She is mad for sexual pleasure but simply
being in her presence nauseates a man.

A nuisance to neighbors by habitual stealing,   55
she likes to eat what is left on altars.
    A prancing, long-maned mare produced
a woman disdainful of work and pain.
She never touches a millstone, lifts
a sieve, empties chamber pots,   60
or sits by the oven, fearing soot.
She makes her husband and poverty friends.
She takes two baths a day and sometimes
three, anointing herself with oil.
She sports a luxurious mane, always   65
freshly combed and covered with flowers.
A woman like this is a pleasant sight
for others, but a bane to a husband, unless
he happens to be a tyrant or king
who prides himself on such possessions.   70
    One from the ape and she is by far
the worst of Zeus' evils for man.
Her facial expressions are hideous; everyone
gets a laugh when she comes to town.
Her neck is short; she hobbles along,   75
all skin and bones, no hips. Pity
the man who embraces such an abomination!
Like an ape, she knows every trick
and scheme, deaf to the laughter she causes.
She would never help a person; her constant   80
goal, the object of all her plans,
is to do the greatest evil she can.
    One from the bee, a blessing to get.
Her alone no criticism fits.
Life with her is green and blooming.   85
Old, she is dear to her husband still.
The mother of a handsome, distinguished brood,
she stands above all other kinds
of women; a godlike grace envelops her.
She does not enjoy sitting with friends   90
to gossip about love and romance.
Such women are Zeus' gift to men,
the best and wisest ones he made.
    All the other breeds exist
and stay with men by Zeus' treachery.   95
Women are the worst evil Zeus
created. They seem to be of use,
but are always their owner's greatest problem.
No one who lives with a woman ever
spends an entirely pleasant day   100

or easily keeps Hunger away,
that hateful guest and hostile god.
When a man plans to be festive at home
on some religious or social occasion,
she takes offense and puts on her helmet.   105
When a woman is present, a man cannot
graciously receive a guest in his home.
The woman who seems most virtuous
commits the most outrageous actions
when her husband looks away, and neighbors   110
rejoice to see another victim.
Everyone praises the woman he has
and finds fault with that of another.
We fail to realize our fates are the same.
Women are Zeus' worst creation,   115
the iron chain shackling our feet
ever since Hades welcomed those men
who died in battle for the sake of a woman. [2]

Zeus the thunderer controls every
outcome, son, and he does what he pleases.
Men are not rational. We live like animals,
a day at a time, unaware of the ends
to which god directs all things,   5
but nursed by hope and faith we push on
in vain. Some wait for dawn,
others a change of season, but there
is not a mortal who does not expect
to be friends with wealth and comfort in a year.   10
Age catches one man first,
before he reaches his goal; others
are crushed by disease or mastered by Ares
and Hades ushers them down below.
Sailors swept away by a hurricane   15
and pounded by dark, salt waves
die in struggle when strength fails,
but men have also applied the noose
to their misery, departing the sunlight freely.
There is no refuge. Death takes   20
countless forms. Pains and grief
exist worse than can be imagined.
I think it wrong to love misfortune,
clinging to life when life is torment.[2] [3]

We have ample time to be dead,
but live just a few hard years. [4]

A dead man should be in our thoughts
for no more than a day—if at all. [5]

Callinus of Ephesus

(7th cent. B.C.)

Callinus was a native of another of the original Ionian colonies, Ephesus. He is the author of just one substantial fragment, which gives us a glimpse of life on the Ionian mainland at the time that Archilochus and Semonides were active in the islands. We hear Callinus urging the youth of Ephesus, in whom we may catch a glimpse of typical pleasure-seeking Ionians, to cast off their lethargy and rouse themselves for war. The details can be reconstructed with probability. Around 700, the Cimmerians, a tribe of Black Sea nomads driven from their homeland by Scythians, entered Asia Minor. Marauders rather than conquerors, their raids punctuate the history of the area for the next hundred years. Early in the century they destroyed Gordium, the capital of Phrygia. In 652, they sacked Sardis and killed Gyges, a king whose wealth was proverbial in Archilochus' time. In Ionia the Cimmerians destroyed Magnesia and threatened other cities. It seems that Callinus urged the Ephesians to prepare to resist the Cimmerian menace, probably not long after the fall of nearby Sardis. His warning was timely. The Cimmerian horde attacked Ephesus, but was driven away.

Callinus' one significant fragment is preserved by Stobaeus. The meter shows that at least one line is missing.

> How long is your nap, lads? When will you show
>   some fight? You should be ashamed
> for neighbors to see you so passive. You lounge in peace,
>   but war grips the land.
> . . . .
>   and fling a spear as he dies.
> What a splendid honor it is to fight the enemy
>   for land, children, and wedded
> wife! Death will come when the spinning Fates
>   decree. Charge straight on,

hold your spear high and cover your chest
    with your shield when the battle starts.
No man can escape his fated death, not even
    one descended from gods.
A soldier can run from the battle, the clash of spears.
    His fate overtakes him at home.
He dies unmourned by the people. But great and small
    weep when another suffers,
for everyone mourns the brave man's death
    and living, he seems a demigod,
a tower that draws all eyes, a single man
    who does the deeds of many. [1]

Mimnermus of Smyrna

(7th cent. B.C.)

Another poet of Ionia, Mimnermus seems to have lived in Smyrna, the Aeolian colony that was taken over by Ionians. It was built at the eastern end of a deep bay, the Gulf of Smyrna. Behind it stretched the Hermus river valley. Sardis rose at the valley's eastern end, fifty miles away. Hence Smyrna blocked Sardis' shortest route to the sea. Herodotus says that the Lydian Gyges raided it early in his reign (ca. 680) and that his grandson Alyattes captured it. Archaeological remains prove that someone did indeed capture the city about 600 by means of a siege mound and left it deserted. In fragment 2, Mimnermus rallies his fellow townsmen against the Lydian threat in tones reminiscent of Callinus. He is apparently invoking the deeds of a hero in the earlier war against Gyges as an example for opposing Alyattes.

In other fragments, Mimnermus laments the brevity of youth and youthful pleasures with powerful directness and simplicity. Mimnermus' poems were published in two books, of which one, probably a miscellany, bore the title "Nanno," a woman's name.

Quotations

In his catalog of drinking vessels, Athenaeus mentions the mythical golden cup in which the Sun sailed on the river of Oceanus (see also Stesichorus fragment 6):

> In *Nanno* Mimnermus says that Helios sails east sleeping in a "couch" of gold designed for this purpose by Hephaestus. That is an allusion to the cup's hollow shape:
>
>> Helios' lot is working every day;
>> there is no rest for him

and his horses from the moment Dawn leaves Oceanus
    and streaks the sky with red.
By night, a winged couch of precious gold,
    luxurious, made by Hephaestus,
carries him sound asleep, skimming the waves,
    from where the Hesperides live
to Ethiopia; here he waits with horses and chariot
    for Dawn to rise in the mist.
Then the son of Hyperion mounts his car. [1]

The remaining fragments are preserved by Stobaeus.

That is not what I hear of his strength and manly
    spirit from elders who saw him
routing the thick ranks of Lydian cavalry,
    a spearman on Hermus' plain.
Pallas Athena never found a flaw
    in his heart's sharp edge
when he sped to the bloody battle, shattering the foremost
    spears of men who hated him
bitterly. But none of them undertook the violent
    task of war with greater
courage: his charge was a beam of sudden sunlight. [2]

Let there be truth between us; all of us have
    a perfect right to it.[1] [3]

What is life or pleasure without golden Aphrodite?
    I would rather be dead than indifferent
to secret love, sweet concessions, bed:
    the most beautiful moments of youth
for men and women. When painful age arrives,
    a man is repulsive and worthless.
Trivial worries batter his mind; seeing
    the sunshine gives no pleasure.
Youths sneer, women turn their backs.
    Some god has cursed old age. [4]

Like leaves that frame spring flowers, rapidly
    growing in the sun's rays,
we briefly enjoy the blossoms of youth, but the gods
    obstruct our vision of evil
and good. Dark demons stand beside us;
    one holds hard age;

the other, death. Youth's harvest is quick,
    fading as daylight does.
And when its time has passed, immediate death
    is better than living. Troubles
throng. One man's exhausted estate no longer
    fends off the ills of poverty;
another has no children and goes to Hades
    desperately wanting them still;
or sickness destroys his spirit. In dispensing evil,
    Zeus is generous to everyone. [5]

The most handsome man, past his prime, is honored
and loved not even by his children. [6]

He gave Tithonus an endless evil: aging,
worse than grievous death. [7]

Sweat drenches my skin and I start to tremble
    when I see adolescence in bloom,
pleasant and fair as it is, since I wish it were more,
    but precious youth is like
a fleeting dream and hideous age, its destroyer,
    hovers overhead from the first;
hateful, worthless, it stupefies the man it envelops,
    blurring his eyes and mind.[2] [8]

Tyrtaeus of Sparta
(7th cent. B.C.)

The continuous political history of mainland Greece begins with Sparta's appearance on the stage; the first Spartan voice is that of Tyrtaeus.

The Spartans were famous for stable government. Their laws, the *rhetra* (covenants), were attributed to the legendary Lycurgus. Full citizens, a small proportion of the population, devoted their lives to military duties. Each citizen owned land, which was farmed by serfs or "helots," and was supported by the income it produced. The constitution was conservative, entrusting virtually all power to two hereditary kings and a council of twenty-eight elders (at least sixty years old). A citizen assembly elected the members of the council and approved or rejected its resolutions, but could not initiate actions. Membership in the assembly was limited to men over thirty who were deemed worthy. One of Tyrtaeus' poems seems to have a been a defense of a reactionary amendment to the *rhetra*, which enabled the council to dismiss the assembly if it attempted independent action (fragments 2 and 4). The respect given to the elderly by the Spartans is reflected in Tyrtaeus' lines about the death of an old soldier (1.19–26).

Tyrtaeus' battle poems are connected with the struggles between Sparta and its neighbor to the west, Messenia. Messenia was conquered by Sparta after the First Messenian War, which lasted for twenty years beginning somewhere between 740 and 730. The Messenians were reduced to serfdom by the Spartans. In the third generation following, about 660 B.C., they revolted and another protracted war occurred. Tyrtaeus seems to have written during this second war. His message was simple: victory at any price. "It is a beautiful thing when a good man falls and dies fighting for his country."

Sparta finally won the Second Messenian War about 640. The effect was to increase greatly the number of serfs controlled by its citizens. This was a mixed blessing, however, since fear of a Helot revolt locked the Spartans into extreme militarism, prevented them from establishing colonies, and eventually deadened other capacities. In the seventh century, Sparta's song and dance were as famous as its warriors. By the fourth, a Spartan was the Greek equivalent of a philistine. In one of Tyrtaeus' most famous fragments (9), he denigrates athletics, wealth, beauty, and rhetoric by comparison to military prowess. Unfortunately for their culture, the Spartans took his message to heart.

Nothing is known about the details of Tyrtaeus' life. Possibly because of Sparta's later backwardness, doubt was raised in antiquity about his birthplace. Pausanias (4.15.6) transmits an Athenian tradition that seems to have gained currency as early as the fourth century (cp. fragment 1). According to this, Tyrtaeus was a lame, befuddled teacher in Athens. During the Second Messenian War, an oracle advised the Spartans to obtain an Athenian adviser. The Athenians gave them Tyrtaeus in bad faith. His "advice" took the form of martial poems, which so restored the troops' morale that they achieved victory.

Quotations

The orator Lycurgus (4th cent. A.D.) preserves Tyrtaeus' most famous poem as part of a speech. He is accusing the defendant of fleeing Athens after its defeat by Philip of Macedon in the battle of Chaeronea, and he says that this behavior falls far short of traditional Athenian courage. This, he notes, was exemplified by Tyrtaeus, whom the Spartans brought from Athens to lead them. Later, they were indifferent to other poets but required their soldiers to listen to his poems before battle so that they would want to die for their country.

It is good to hear these verses to learn how people gained glory among the Spartans:

It is a beautiful thing when a good man falls
and dies fighting for his country.

The worst pain is leaving one's city and fertile
    fields for the life of a beggar,
wandering with mother, old father, little
    children, and wedded wife.
The man beaten by need and odious poverty
    is detested everywhere he goes,
a disgrace to his family and noble appearance, trailed
    by every dishonor and evil.
If no one takes care of the wanderer or gives him
    honor, respect, or pity,
we must fight to the death for our land and children, giving
    no thought to lengthening life.
Fight in a stubborn, close array, my boys!
    Never waver or retreat!
Feel your anger swell. There is no place
    in combat for love of life.
Older soldiers, whose knees are not so light,
    need you to stand and protect them.
An aging warrior cut down in the vanguard of battle
    disgraces the young. His head
is white, his beard is grey, and now he is spilling
    his powerful spirit in dust,
naked, clutching his bloody groin: a sight
    for shame and anger. But youthful
warriors always look good, until the blossom
    withers. Men gape
at them in life and women sigh, and dying
    in combat they are handsome still.
Now is the time for a man to stand, planting
    his feet and biting his lip. [1]

Diodorus Siculus (1st cent. B.C.) wrote a forty-volume history of the world. While volumes six through eleven are lost, excerpts from them have been recovered from other manuscripts. A tenth-century collection of quotations from Diodorus' lost books has provided fragment 2 below. A marginal note says that they were oracles given to Lycurgus, Sparta's legendary legislator—*not* the fourth-century orator. The "oracles" overlap with Plutarch's quotations of Tyrtaeus in fragment 4 and are attributed to Tyrtaeus for that reason.

Lord of the silver bow, far-striking Apollo
    from his wealthy temple commanded
the kings, caretakers of lovely Sparta, honored
    by the gods, and the noblest elders

to direct the council. On common men he enjoined
  obedience to the covenants undistorted,
noble speech, justice in all their deeds,
  and adopting no crooked counsel.
He promised that victory and power for all would follow.
  Such were Phoebus' revelations. [2]

In his geography, Strabo (1st cent. B.C./1st cent. A.D.) mentions the
fact that

Messene fell to the Spartans after a war of nineteen years, as Tyrtaeus
says:

For nineteen years, spearmen,
our fathers' fathers battled with stubborn hearts
  to win her. Her people abandoned
their rich estates in the twentieth year, leaving
  the high hills of Ithome. [3]

In his life of the Spartan legislator Lycurgus, Plutarch gives a slightly
different version of fragment 2 together with its political background.
He explains that originally the Spartan assembly only had the right
to ratify or reject the proposals framed by the kings and elders. In
time, it began to amend proposals, thus in effect writing original
legislation. Hence kings Polydorus and Theopompus added to the
rhetra a clause authorizing kings or elders to dismiss assemblies try-
ing to pass "crooked," i.e., amended, resolutions. Furthermore,

they persuaded the city that they had inserted this clause with divine
sanction, as Tyrtaeus mentions somewhere in these words:

Hearing Phoebus, they carried his oracles and perfect
  pronouncements home from Pytho.
The kings, caretakers of lovely Sparta, honored
  by the gods, and the noblest elders
should direct the council. On common men he enjoined
  obedience to the covenants undistorted. [4]

The geographer Pausanias (2nd cent. A.D.) inserts a history of the
Messenian Wars into his description of southern Greece. In introduc-
ing the topic, he mentions that a Messenian hero, Aristomenes, was

falsely credited by a historian named Myron with killing the Spartan king Theopompus.

> But we know that Theopompus did not die in battle or in any way before the end of the war. It was he who brought the war to a conclusion. My evidence is the elegy of Tyrtaeus, saying:
>
>> our king, Theopompus, dear to the gods, through whom
>> we captured Messene the spacious. [5]

Pausanias' account ends with the terms of surrender imposed on the Messenians after the second war: they swore to deliver half of their farm produce to Sparta and to attend the funerals of Spartan leaders in black clothing. He adds,

> Tyrtaeus wrote the following lines on the harsh punishments they inflicted on the Messenians:
>
>> Like overloaded, worn-out mules,
>> they bring to their masters, by painful compulsion, half
>> of everything their fields produce. [6]
>
> That they were forced to participate in mourning is made clear in this couplet:
>
>> men and their wives, mourning their masters whenever
>> one was overtaken by death. [7]

Finally, Stobaeus preserves two fragments.

> Courage, children of unconquered Heracles! Zeus
>> has not yet turned his back.
> Fear no multitude. Never panic. Push
>> your shield in the enemy's face,
> despising life and loving death's dark
>> demons like rays of the sun.
> You know war's harsh temperament and how
>> Ares works destruction.
> You have joined in retreat and pursuit, young fighters;
>> you have had your fill of both.
> When men stand side by side, not flinching
>> from hand-to-hand fights at the front,

some die, but they save their people. When men run away,
    all their virtue is lost.
No one could name every evil that comes
    to a man in such disgrace.
Though cleaving the back of a man in flight in the heat
    of combat gives no pleasure,[1]
the corpse fixed to the ground by a spear thrown
    from behind lies in disgrace.
Now is the time for a man to stand, planting
    his feet and biting his lip,
to hide his body, ankles to neck, behind
    a shield's big belly,
to jab on the right with his strong spear and shake
    his helmet's fearsome crest.
Violent acts teach warfare better
    than cowering out of range.
March to the front, close with the enemy, strike
    with spear or sword and take him.
A man who holds spear or sword must fight
    that way: toe to toe,
shield to shield, crest to crest, helmet
    to helmet, breastplate to breastplate.
You soldiers who are lightly armed can each
    find a shield to crouch by,
throw your stones and spears, keeping close
    to men in heavy armor. [8]

I would not commemorate a man for his excellent
    running or wrestling, not
if he had the size and strength of the Cyclopes, beat
    Thracian Boreas running,
was fairer of form than Tithonus, richer than Midas
    and Cinyras, more kingly
than Tantalid Pelops, had a tongue that spoke
    sweet as Adrastus and every
other distinction, but lacked furious courage.
    In war, no man is good
unless he faces blood and death, taking
    a stand in enemy reach.
That is excellence; *that* is the noblest contest
    a young man can win.
. The city and all of its people gain when a man
    takes an unflinching stand
in battle, gives no thought to flight but calmly
    wagers life and spirit

with a cheerful word to the soldier beside him. In war,
    that is a "good man."
He quickly turns the bristling enemy ranks;
    his determination stems the tide
of battle. Though he may fall and die, struck
    in the chest a hundred times
despite his shield and breastplate, he leaves his fame
    to his city, people, and father.
Old men and youths have tears in their eyes,
    the city staggers with grief,
but his tomb and children are famous, even his children's
    children and later descendants.
His name and legend never die. Lying
    in the earth, he becomes immortal,
whoever is killed by Ares, heroically standing
    and fighting for land and children;
and the man who escapes the leveling demon and earns
    the victorious warrior's boast
accepts congratulation from young and old, and many
    joys smooth his earthly
journey. With age, he becomes a prominent counselor.
    No one would cheat or insult him.
Older, younger, the same in years—everyone
    yields his place on the benches.
Climb the hill of virtue, soldier; never
    soften your warrior's heart. [9]

Alcman of Sparta

(7th cent B.C.)

Alcman's fragments embody the doomed lighter side of the Spartan character. He is the earliest choral poet whose work survives in appreciable quantity. His career belongs to the late seventh century, in the afterglow of Sparta's final victory over Messenia. As in the case of Tyrtaeus, his birthplace was a matter of controversy in antiquity. Some scholars said that he came from Sardis, apparently on the basis of the poem from which fragments 4 and 14 are taken. In its present state, however, this evidence is weak. It is unclear whether the relevant verb represents the first person or third person. Even if the first person ("I came from the heights of Sardis") was intended, there is a good chance that the poem was not really autobiographical.

Alcman's poems give us an intriguing glimpse of Spartan culture in the seventh century. His longest fragment (2) and several shorter ones (1, 12, 13) come from *partheneia*, songs to be sung by choruses of virgins (*parthenoi*) at religious festivals. Fragment 2 gives us an idea of what a complete *partheneion* was like. It contains a mythical narrative, which is now poorly preserved, followed by lines in which the chorus talks about its own concerns. It seems to be competing in singing, dancing, and beauty with at least one other chorus. Its members are confident of victory because of the beauty of their leader, Hagesichora, and her assistant, Agido. As a poet, Alcman is parochial, composing for an audience personally acquainted with Hagesichora, Agido, and the others, but his metaphors and similes have universal appeal. The erotic terms in which his maidens speak of each other are worth considering as evidence that female homosexuality was common in Archaic Greece, even beyond Lesbos.

It is difficult to classify the other fragments. Apparently, Alcman wrote songs for various occasions. One ancient author considered

him the inventor of the love song (fragment 10), another indication
of how much the atmosphere in Sparta changed over the years.

Papyrus Fragments

An Oxyrhynchus papyrus (1st cent. B.C./1st cent. A.D.) preserves
several lines of a maidens' song by Alcman. Members of the chorus
are praising their leader, Astymeloisa, in amorous terms.

> More surely
> than sleep or death her gaze dissolves me,
> and not without reason, sweet as she is.
>
> Astymeloisa has no words for me,
> holding the holy crown,
> like a shooting star across
> the radiant sky,
> a golden bough, a gentle. . . . [1]

The famous Louvre Papyrus (1st cent. A.D.) found by the French
Egyptologist Auguste Mariette in 1855 contains the longest extant
segment of pre-Classical choral poetry, a portion of another maidens'
song by Alcman. The beginning of the poem is completely lost and
the first thirty-five lines of the extant text are too mutilated for con-
tinuous translation. They seem to have told the story of the destruc-
tion of minor heroes, the sons of Hippocöon, by Heracles and Castor
and Polydeuces. Lines 102–4 are not preserved, but a *coronis* (wavy
line) after line 104 shows that the poem ended at that point.

Several passages are difficult to interpret and have been frequently
discussed. My translation incorporates Martin West's cogent inter-
pretation.[1] The song honors a deity known only as *Aotis* (Dawn-
goddess). A puzzling reference to one Aenesimbrota makes sense if
we assume that she is a woman who trades in love potions and spells.

> Divine retribution is real;   36
> blessed is he
> who weaves a prudent and tearless
> day. But I sing
> of Agido's brilliance. She draws   40
> my gaze like the sun
> she invokes as a shining witness;
> but our dance's glorious

leader will not have another word of praise   45
or blame, for she thinks that she herself
is the one to notice, a thoroughbred
in the common herd, a thundering,
muscular steed, the kind
you dream of, dozing in the shade.

Picture an Adriatic courser,   50
but above the mane
of my cousin, Hagesichora, hovers
a golden sheen,
and her cool smooth brow,
like silver—but why   55
elaborate? Simply say,
"This is Hagesichora!"

Whoever races Agido in beauty will seem
a Scythian steed trailing a Lydian.
For rivals rise up but dimly,   60
like Pleiades at dawn, and our light
is bright as the star Sirius
framed by ambrosial night.

This confidence does not depend
on plenteous purples,   65
the spangled, golden snakes
on our wrists, Lydian
headbands, pride of dewy-
eyed girls,
Nanno's tresses, Areta,   70
though she looks divine,
Sylacis or Clëesisera, nor will you ever run
for a magic spell to Aenesimbrota's, crying:
"Let Astaphis be mine!
Let Philylla, beloved Damareta   75
and Vianthemis look my way!"
But, "Hagesichora is making me weak!"

That girl with lovely ankles,
Hagesichora, is gone.
She stands at Agido's side,   80
commending our celebration.
Hear their prayers, O gods,
masters of success
and fulfillment. My leader, I too
would speak, a maiden   85
whose song does nothing but grate, like that of an owl
on a rafter, and yet my heart is passionate

to please Aotis, who heals
our pains, but only by following
Hagesichora have maidens won   90
their way to the peace they long for.

A chariot race is the same:
the trace-horse leads
the team, and on ships the rowers
obey the pilot.   95
The song that we ten children
sing is not
as sweet as the Sirens', for they
are divine and eleven.
Our voices more closely resemble a swan on the banks   100
of the Xanthos, but the lovely blond braids. . . .[2]

Quotations

Antigonus of Carystus (3rd cent. B.C.), author of a book of "won-
ders," cites lines by Alcman in support of an improbable assertion:

When [male halcyons] grow weak with age and are no longer able to fly,
the females take them on their wings and carry them. A passage by
Alcman alludes to this; for he says that being weak with age he is unable
to move around with his choruses or the dancing of the maidens:

Strong and sweet your song flows, maidens,
but my limbs can bear me no longer. *Balee! Balee!*
Make me a kingfisher skimming the crests with my mates,
a holy, sea-purple bird with heart untroubled. [3]

In describing western Greece, Strabo (1st cent. B.C./1st cent. A.D.)
enumerates the peoples dwelling in Acarnania, a rural district.
Among them,

Apollodorus says that the "Erysicheans" mentioned by Alcman are
thought to live in its interior:

Scarcely an Erysichean shepherd,
he hailed from the heights of Sardis. [4]

See fragment 14 for the beginning of this passage, which is the basis
of the theory that Alcman was a native of Lydia.

In his Homeric lexicon, Apollonius the Sophist (1st cent. B.C./1st cent. A.D.) says that the term "beasts" (*theria*) properly applies to animals like lions and wolves, "serpents" (*herpeta*) to snakes, and "monsters" (*knodala*) to great fish and other predators in the sea. For example,

Alcman makes these distinctions, saying:

Mountain peaks, ravines, headlands,
cascading torrents sleep;
the serpents dark earth breeds,
beasts of the hills, the race of bees,
monsters that plumb the purple sea,
and long-winged flocks are sleeping too. [5]

From Hephaestion's *Handbook:*

Aphrodite is innocent; Eros, her driven child,
tramples the blooming meadow you should not touch. [6]

Athenaeus first cites Alcman when the conversation turns to the topic of gluttony.

The poet Alcman reveals his own gluttony in his third book in these verses:

My gift to you sometime shall be
a tripod bowl for a heap of food,
unfired now but soon to be full
of the simmering soup omnivorous Alcman
loves when the year turns cold.
He does not care for gourmet dishes,
but common things, the fare the people
prefer. [7]

He also stresses his gluttony in his fifth book when he says:

He created three seasons,
summer, winter, and fall,
then added a fourth, the spring,
when everything blossoms, except
enough to eat. [8]

Athenaeus also cites Alcman in the course of his catalog of drinking vessels. He says that the *skyphos* is a large cup used primarily by peasants, e.g., Homer's pig herd, Eumaeus (*Odyssey* 14.112).

And Alcman says:

> As the gods smiled down on your torchlight revel
> high in the hills, you often took
> a golden vessel, big as the cup [*skyphos*]
> that a shepherd carries, brimmed it with lion's
> milk and made a smooth cheese for Hermes. [9]

Finally, Athenaeus preserves the tradition that Alcman was a pioneer in erotic song.

> According to Chamaeleon, Archytas, the expert on music, says Alcman
> was the first to compose love songs and to publish licentious music, being
> inclined in his habits towards women and music of this sort. Thus he says
> in one of his songs:

> > Once more by the Cyprian's will, Eros
> > floods my heart with sweetness and warmth. [10]

> Chamaeleon adds that Alcman fell madly in love with Megalostrata, a
> poetess, whose conversation was able to attract lovers. About her he
> wrote:

> > Fair Megalostrata, fortunate
> > maid, revealed the gift
> > the Muses sweetly gave her. [11]

A fifth-century A.D. commentator on Hermogenes' rhetoric uses lines from Alcman to illustrate what a strophe is, i.e., a metrical unit consisting of two or more similar or dissimilar lines:

> As in Alcman,

> > Calliope, Muse, daughter of Zeus,
> > start the stories we love and put
> > passion in our song and graceful dancing. [12]

> This strophe consists of three equivalent dactylic lines. Others consist of
> dissimilar lines, like the following:

Come ever tuneful, silver-voiced
Muse, guide
these maids through a new and various song. [13]

Finally, Stephanus of Byzantium (6th cent. A.D.) gives the beginning
of fragment 4 in his entry on Erysiche in his geographical lexicon:

The man was no field hand,
not ill at ease in educated
circles, not a Thessalian,
scarcely an Erysichean shepherd. [14]

Solon of Athens

(7th/6th cent. B.C.)

We hear little of Sparta's great rival, Athens, in the seventh century. Two major events typical of the age are recorded. A noble named Cylon tried to make himself tyrant of the city but was driven out; some followers who had taken refuge in the temple of Athena were illegally executed. A few years later, Draco published his written legal code. A few clauses survive. The code was reputedly harsh, but any written code was an advance in the rights of the common man.

The earliest events in Athens that we can study in detail are connected with the city's great poet and statesman, Solon, who flourished early in the sixth century. In 594/3, he was given the power to rewrite Athens' laws. The lower classes looked to his reforms for relief from various injustices, while the privileged hoped to prevent a *coup d'état* by a tyrant. We do not know why Solon was the one man chosen. He was a noble, but not particularly wealthy. We are told that he had become a hero by using poetry to rally Athenian resolve, so that they might gain control of the island of Salamis from Megara (fragments 20 and 21).

Solon's reforms offered something to all three elements in the state. What the nobles feared most was the loss of land; Solon refused to confiscate any. The Athenian poor had two main problems. Many were *hectemoroi* (sixth-parters): apparently, they were obliged to give one sixth of their harvests to a quasi-landlord. It is not known how this came about. Possibly in unsettled times small farmers became *hectemoroi* in return for protection from more powerful neighbors. By 594/3, the institution was resented. Solon abolished it and was proud of having "freed" Athenian soil from the markers that designated sixth-parters' fields.

The other problem was debt. When they borrowed, the poor used themselves as collateral. If they defaulted on a loan, they were enslaved to their creditors. Coinage was first introduced into the Greek world in Solon's generation; Athens did not yet coin its own money. Indebtedness was probably not as prevalent as it was to become in money economies. Still, one of Solon's essential reforms was to make debts secured by personal freedom illegal; he also claims to have freed a number of enslaved debtors in Athens and to have returned others who had been sold or had fled abroad.

The newly rich were probably Solon's most influential supporters. Previously, the nobles, known in Athens as "Eupatrids," had enjoyed the usual monopoly of political power. Nine archons, the chief magistrates, were elected from their number annually. After their year in office, they became members of the Areopagus council. An assembly of all citizens met under extraordinary circumstances, but normally all judicial, executive, and legislative functions were left to the Areopagus and the archons. Around 600 B.C., Athens began exporting olive oil to the shores of the Black Sea. Perhaps the profits enriched non-Eupatrid landowners who then began to agitate against their exclusion from political offices. Solon divided the citizens into four groups on the basis of income. All members of the first group and possibly the second, regardless of family connections, became eligible to serve as archons and join the Areopagus. Solon also created a new council of four hundred, whose function was framing proposals to go to the popular assembly. Membership in the new council, restricted to the top two or three income groups, represented another avenue of political power for the non-Eupatrid rich. Another change benefited both the poor and the newly rich. Previously, all judicial proceedings were in the hands of the Eupatrid archons and the Areopagus. By Solon's laws all citizens could appeal their decisions to the assembly: they obtained the right to be tried by a jury of peers.

After framing his laws, Solon is supposed to have left Athens for ten years to escape pressure to amend them. When he returned to Athens, he realized that a certain Pisistratus had designs on tyrannical power, and Solon tried in vain to rouse the Athenians to oppose him (fragments 22–24). Pisistratus did become the tyrant in Athens, but a benign one. He treated Solon with respect and enforced his laws.

Quotations in the *Athenaion Politeia* Papyrus

Aristotle (4th cent. B.C.) and his students are said to have compiled the constitutional histories of 158 city-states. None of these treatises seemed to have survived until the discovery in 1890 of four papyrus scrolls containing the most important such treatise, the *Constitution of the Athenians* (*Athenaion Politeia*), almost complete. It is not known whether Aristotle himself or one of his students actually wrote the work.

An early section of the text summarizes Solon's reforms and contains seven significant quotations from his poetry. The account begins with the statement that the lower classes were oppressed under Draco's laws. Then,

> the people rose up against the aristocrats. The strife was violent and the two sides fought each other for a long time. Finally, they chose Solon as arbitrator and leader and handed the constitution over to him after he composed the elegy beginning:
>
> > I understand the crisis, and it fills my heart with pain
> >   to see the decline of Ionia's
> > eldest land. [1]
>
> In it he argues against each side on behalf of the other and urges them to end their long-standing quarrel. Solon was by nature and reputation one of the leading citizens but a member of the middle class by property and business dealings. This is the testimony of other writers and he himself provides evidence in his poems when he urges the rich not to be greedy:
>
> > You who have gained wealth in excess, calm
> >   your desire and temper ambition;
> > for we shall not obey, nor will these matters
> >   fall out however suits you. [2]

At this point, the author lists the Solonian reforms that were especially democratic: prohibition of debts secured by one's person; the right of anyone to indict another for an injury (not just the injured party); and the right of appeal to popular juries.

After Solon published his reforms,

> both sides turned against him because his settlement was not what they expected; the people thought that he would redistribute all property and

the aristocrats thought that he would return things to their previous
state or make minor changes. He opposed both. Even though it was
possible for him to take whichever side he preferred and become a
tyrant, he chose to hold out against both sides, thereby preserving the
state and giving the best legislation possible. All other sources agree
that this is what happened, and he himself recalls the events in these
words:

> I gave the people the rights they needed without
>   stealing or adding honor.
> Thanks to my precautions, the powerful and wealthy
>   suffered no disgrace.
> I lent both sides my shield's protection, conceding
>   to neither an unjust victory. [3]

He also describes the proper treatment of the people in these words:

> The people follow those leaders best who neither
>   tolerate license nor oppress.
> When men of bad character prosper greatly,
>   satisfaction turns to arrogance. [4]

Elsewhere he speaks of those who desired a redistribution of land:

> They came for plunder with rich expectation,
> hoping for wealth when I revealed
> the harsh intention of my soothing words.
> Mistaken then, they resent me now,
> casting hostile, crooked looks   5
> unfairly. With the gods, I did what I promised,
> and other worthwhile acts, but refused
> to use tyrannical force to give
> the lowborn an equal share of the fatherland. [5]

He speaks in the same vein about his cancellation of debts and the
liberation of slaves on account of the *seisachtheia*.[1]

> Why did I stop before I reached
> the goals for which I assembled the people?
> She who bore the gods of Olympus,
> Earth, greatest and best, whom I cleansed
> of mortgage stones, planted everywhere,   5
> shall testify for me in the court of Time.
> Then she was slave, now she is free.
> I restored to Athens, their god-built home,
> many who were sold abroad, sometimes
> by crooked judgments, or voluntarily fled

a crushing burden of debt and wandered
so far they lost their Attic accents.
Others I freed from the shame of slavery
in the heart of Athens, where once they trembled
at a master's whim. And though I gained
my ends by force, I melded Power
with Justice and did what I promised to do.
The laws I wrote were the same for lowborn
and noble; both were straightened by Justice.
If a stupid or greedy man had held
the goad like me, he would not have controlled
the people. The city would surely have had
an abundance of widows, if I had permitted
either side to do what it wanted
or approved the plans of either faction.
So keeping my guard in every direction,
I whirled like a wolf circled by dogs. [6]

He chided both parties for the criticism in these words:

If one may criticize the people in public,
they never would have seen the things
I gave them, even in dreams. . . .
Men of superior status and power
should praise me and call me a friend. . . .

Because, he says, if anyone else had received the same power

he would not have stopped the people until
they shook the milk and drained the cream,
but I stood unmoved as a pillar between
opposing armies. [7]

Quotations in Manuscripts

The orator Demosthenes (4th cent. B.C.) had a poem by Solon read
into the record in the course of a speech indicting his rival Aeschines
for treason. Both men had been members of a group of Athenians
sent to Macedon to negotiate with King Philip. Aeschines allegedly
accepted a bribe from Philip to support his policies. In the course of
defending himself, Aeschines criticized the flamboyant speaking
style of one of his other prosecutors, saying that he should have kept
his hands folded inside his robe as Solon is represented doing in
statues. (*Nothing* was deemed irrelevant in ancient Greek trials.) De-

mosthenes turns this point against Aeschines by contrasting his al-
leged treason with Solon's patriotism. He alludes to the tradition that
Solon feigned madness, wearing a skullcap as if sick, when he first
rallied the Athenians to invade Salamis. He says,

It is not necessary to speak with your hands inside your robe, Aeschines,
but it is necessary to keep them hidden when you are an ambassador. In
Macedonia you held them out and turned them over to our disgrace. You
speak solemnly, declaim some wretched little speeches, exercise your
voice and think that you will not pay the price for so many great crimes,
if you just go around with a skull cap on and abuse me. Now read:

> Our city will never perish by decree of Zeus
>   or whim of the immortals; such
> is the great-hearted protector, child of thunder, who holds
>   her hands over us: Athena.
> But by thoughtless devotion to money, the citizens are willing
>   to destroy our great city.
> Our leaders' minds are unjust; soon they will suffer
>   the pangs of great arrogance.
> They cannot control their greed and enjoy the cheerful
>   feast at hand in peace.
> . . . .
> Their wealth depends on crime.
> . . . .
> They seize and steal at random
> without regard for the holy, the public good,
>   or the sacred foundations of Justice,
> who is silent but knows present and past, and comes
>   for full retribution in time.
> The deadly infection spreads throughout the city,[2]
>   rushing it into slavery,
> which wakens internal strife and war that kills
>   so many beautiful youths.
> Malicious conspiracies easily ruin a city,
>   though the people love it dearly.
> These are the evils stalking the people: many
>   impoverished leave for foreign
> soil, bound and sold in chains of disgrace.
> . . . .
> The public evil visits every home;
>   undeterred by courtyard gates,
> it leaps the high hedge and finds its man,
>   though he runs to his bedroom to hide.

My heart bids me to teach the Athenians that lawless
    behavior is the bane of a city,
but respect for law spreads order and beauty;
    it shackles the legs of the unjust,
smooths and moderates, diminishes arrogance and withers
    delusion's burgeoning blossoms;
it straightens crooked judgments, humbles pride,
    halts partisanship and the anger
born of faction. Everything righteous and wise
    depends on respect for the law. [8]

Now you have heard, Athenians, what Solon says of men like Aeschines
and of the gods that protect our city.

Philo (1st cent. B.C./1st cent. A.D.), a Jewish theologian of Alexandria,
cites Solon in a commentary on Genesis. He says that God's resting
on the seventh day reflects the marvellous qualities of the number
seven. Indeed, a man's life consists of a succession of seven-year
periods.

Solon, the Athenians' lawgiver, described these periods in elegiac verses:

At seven, an immature boy loses the row
    of teeth he grew in infancy.
When god completes another seven years,
    there are signs of coming adulthood.
His limbs still grow in the third seven, and a beard
    blossoms on his changing skin.
In the fourth seven, his strength is greatest, which men
    consider proof of virtue.
The time to think of marriage and having children
    comes in the fifth seven.
In the sixth, the mind is fit in every way;
    its wishes are no longer lawless.
He reaches his best in thought and speech in the seventh
    and eighth, for fourteen years.
In the ninth, he is able but less inclined to strive
    for greatness in speech and wisdom.
And if someone completes a tenth seven, death
    will not befall him prematurely. [9]

In his life of Solon, Plutarch quotes Solon's poetry mostly to illustrate
his values. For example,

He is agreed to have been a lover of wisdom, who when he had aged said
that as he grew older he was always learning. He did not admire wealth.
He said that a man who owned

> . . . silver and gold in abundance,
>   acres of wheat-bearing land,
> horses and mules is no richer than one whose belly,
>   sides, and feet are well,
> who sometimes enjoys a boy or woman and lives
>   in harmony with his age.[3] [10]

Elsewhere he said:

> I long for wealth, but not unjustly gained;
>   justice always comes.[4] [11]

Like the author of *Constitution of the Athenians*, Plutarch infers that
Solon did not consider himself wealthy:

> That he considered himself poor rather than rich is clear from the follow-
> ing verses:
>
> > Though many scoundrels are rich and good men
> >   struggle, we would not trade
> > virtue for wealth. Quality is permanent; riches
> >   go from man to man.[5] [12]

Plutarch respects Solon as an ethical and political thinker, but

in physics, he is simplistic and primitive, as is clear from these verses:

> Sleet and snow descend from cloud, thunder
>   from lightning's blinding flash;
> the winds churn up the sea, but when there is none
>   to disturb it, nothing is smoother. [13]

In fact, Solon was speaking figuratively about the danger of tyranny;
see fragment 23 for a different version of this passage.

Plutarch stresses the notion that Solon could have made himself
tyrant of Athens but refused to do so as a matter of principle, despite
the urging of his friends:

None of [his friends'] arguments shook Solon's resolve. We are told he said to his friends that tyrannical power is a lovely spot but there is no way to leave it. In his poems, he addresses this to Phokos:

> That I spared
> my country and refused to soil my honor
> by wrapping myself in tyranny and force,
> causes no shame; it is what distinguishes me
> from all the others. [14]

From this we infer that he had a considerable reputation before his legislation. This is how he has described the ridicule to which many people subjected him when he refused to become a tyrant:

> "Solon was a shallow, stupid man.
> He rejected the gifts gods gave him.
> Amazed by his catch, he lacked the courage
> and brains to pull in the heavy net.
> For power, wealth, and a single day
> as Athens' tyrant, I would be skinned
> alive and let my descendants perish." [15]

Plutarch also cites Solon in a "Dialogue on Love." This is the report of a debate between friends as to whether a handsome young man should marry a wealthy widow. The negative speaker is a champion of homosexual relationships, which according to him tend to be spiritual. To support the point he notes that Solon outlawed homosexual relationships involving slaves, because their involvement reduced such affairs to the level of mere physical pleasure, "like copulation with women." He is interrupted at this point by his heterosexual opponent, who says,

> I am glad you mentioned Solon. We can use him as an example of the erotic man.

> 'til he loves a boy in the bloom of youth, yearning
>   for thighs and sweet lips. [16]

And to Solon we can add Aeschylus saying:

> You did not respect my reverence for your thighs,
>   ungrateful for our many kisses.

Others just find these men laughable when they exhort lovers to gaze at thighs and buttocks like priests with a victim or seers, but I also view this as a great argument in favor of women.

His point is that it is seemly for women to submit to men's sexual desires but that it is ludicrous and unnatural for other men to do so. Therefore, heterosexual relationships are more likely to foster true friendship. And so, he concludes,

I think that Solon wrote those lines when he was young and "full of seed," as Plato puts it [*Laws* 8.839 B]. When he was older he wrote:

The quest for pleasure is dear to me now: the works
of Aphrodite, Dionysus, and the Muses. [17]

It sounds as if he had steered his life away from the stress and storm of pederasty to the calm waters of marriage and philosophy.[6]

Clement of Alexandria (2nd/3rd cent. A.D.) adduces a couplet from Solon to explain why Jesus compared the Kingdom of Heaven to yeast [Matt. 13.33]: it is unseen and affects everything that contains it.

As Solon very wisely wrote with reference to God:

It is difficult to see wisdom's farthest boundary,
where the ends of all things lie. [18]

Later, commenting on Isaiah 40.13 ("Who has known the mind of the lord? What counsellor was with him?"), Clement says,

Solon the Athenian, imitating Hesiod, put it well:

We can in no way apprehend the mind of the gods. [19]

Diogenes Laertius (3rd cent. A.D.) wrote short biographies of philosophers, including Solon. He says that Solon's greatest service to the Athenians was rallying them to fight Megara for possession of Salamis.

He rushed into the agora with a garland on his head. There he had his elegy on Salamis read to the Athenians by a herald and he roused them up. They made war on the Megarians again and were victorious because of Solon. The verses that especially touched the Athenians were these:

> Then let me change my race and be Pholegandrian
>   or Sicinite, Athenian no more;
> for here is what people will soon be saying: "Attica,
>   land of Salamis-ceders."[20]

And:

> We shall go to Salamis to fight for the lovely island
>   and shed our bitter disgrace. [21]

We also learn that in later years Solon rushed into the assembly wearing armor to warn the Athenians that Pisistratus was planning to install a tyranny.

The council, consisting of Pisistratus' supporters, declared that he was insane, which led him to recite this:

> A little time will show how mad I am,
>   when Truth appears on the scene. [22]

The following are the verses in which he foretold the development of Pisistratus' tyranny:

> Sleet and snow descend from cloud, thunder
>   from lightning's blinding flash,
> and a city's destruction from "great men," when a despot
>   enslaves unwary people.[7] [23]

Diogenes adds that Solon sent the following verses to Athens when he learned that Pisistratus had actually taken over:

> Place no blame on the gods when your own evil
>   causes bitter suffering.
> You gave those men their power by granting guards;
>   that is the cause of your slavery.
> Each of you walks with a fox's gait, but exhibits
>   the same mental infirmity:
> you consider the flatterer's tongue and shifting speech,
>   not his actual deed. [24]

Stobaeus preserves two fragments. The first is traditionally known as the Hymn to the Muses.

Wondrous children of Memory and Olympian Zeus,
    Pierian Muses, hear me!
Give me prosperity, sent by the gods, and constant,
    good reputation with men.
Make me sweet to friends and bitter to foes,   5
    honored and feared in turn.
I long for riches, but not unjustly gained;
    justice always arrives.
A man can depend on wealth given by gods;
    it is solid from base to peak.   10
But wealth that men extort gets out of control.
    A reluctant attendant, constrained
by unjust actions, it quickly mixes with Ruin,
    which spreads like a little fire:
a trivial matter at first, its end is grievous.   15
    Violent deeds go wrong.
Zeus watches how everything ends and suddenly
    acts, like the wind that scatters
clouds in spring and stirs the depths of the sea,
    constantly swelling, topples   20
fair buildings on land, reaches heaven,
    and clears the sky to view.
The beautiful strength of the sun brightens the earth;
    no cloud remains in sight.
Such is Zeus' vengeance. He is not like a mortal: 25
    quick to anger at every
provocation, but a wicked heart never escapes him;
    all is revealed in the end.
They pay at once or later. Some escape
    the attack of fate themselves,   30
But it surely comes at last, and blameless children
    or later descendants pay.
Good and bad, we mortals all believe
    our expectations will be fulfilled,
until we suffer. Then we weep. Before,   35
    we enjoy our mindless hopes.
The person racked by illness persuades himself
    that he will soon be well.
The coward thinks that he is a hero; the homely
    man is handsome to himself;   40
the pauper, forced to do the works of poverty,
    fully expects to be wealthy.
They scurry here and there. One sails the sea
    and dreams of a rich homecoming.
Over the deep he defies the dangerous winds   45
    with little regard for life.

Men of the crooked plough spend the year
    furrowing the wooded earth.
The master of Athena's skills or those of Hephaestus
    makes a living by hand.   50
Another has learned the gifts of the Olympian Muses
    and the measure of beautiful art.
Far-shooting Apollo can make a man a prophet,
    who sees danger afar
with the help of the gods, but neither omens nor sacrifice   55
    wholly ward off Fate.
Some do the work of Paeon, god of medicine:
    physicians, whose toil is endless.
Small pain often leads to great,
    and drugs bring no relief,   60
but a man in the throes of terrible illness is sometimes
    cured by a touch of the hand.
Fate brings disaster and good fortune,
    gifts of the gods, unavoidable.
Every journey has a risk; no one knows   65
    at the outset where he will land.
A person striving for excellence suddenly slips
    into the depths of ruin,
while a god gives luck to a careless worker,
    saving him from his mistakes.   70
In the race for wealth, there is no finish line.
    The richest of us are straining
to double our possessions. What could satisfy us all?
    The immortals grant wealth,
but wealth precedes Ruin, which takes its toll   75
    whenever Zeus decides. [25]

No mortal is "blessed"; every human being
    the sun sees suffers. [26]

Alcaeus of Lesbos

(7th/6th cent. B.C.)

The poetry of Alcaeus gives us a different perspective on the politics of Archaic Greece. The scene is Mytilene, the main city of the island of Lesbos and one of the original Aeolic settlements.

For centuries Mytilene had been ruled by the Penthilid clan, supposed descendants of Orestes. The head of the clan was the king of the city. The last Penthilid king was killed and the clan's power broken in the second half of the seventh century. Thereafter, other aristocrats competed for power. The struggle led to the emergence of three successive tyrants. The first, Melanchrus, was overthrown between 612 and 609 by a faction that included a tyrant-to-be named Pittacus and Alcaeus' brothers. Apparently, Alcaeus himself was too young to participate. The second tyrant was named Myrsilus. It is not known exactly when he gained power or how long he kept it. Alcaeus' fragment 6 implies that the poet and a group of comrades including Pittacus laid plans to overthrow Myrsilus, but Pittacus switched sides at the last minute. Some of the conspirators lost their lives in an ensuing battle, while others including Alcaeus went into exile, cursing Pittacus.

Eventually, Myrsilus died. Alcaeus was ecstatic (fragment 15), but his joy was short-lived. The Mytilenaean assembly voted to give Pittacus supreme power, making him an anomaly—an elected tyrant. He governed the city well from 590 to 580, finally allowing Alcaeus' faction to return, and he then enjoyed ten years of retirement.

At some point in Alcaeus' lifetime, Mytilene fought Athens for control of the coast east of Lesbos, ancient Troy, and vicinity. After one battle, Alcaeus wrote a poem in which he, like Archilochus, claimed to have thrown his shield away to save his life. His poetry is also the likeliest source of a legendary feat by Pittacus: defeating an Athenian general, an Olympic victor named Phrynon, in single combat.

Alcaeus is most often remembered as the earliest known poet to use the ship-of-state metaphor (1, 8, 9): Myrsilus' growing power is a storm that threatens to sink Mytilene. In general, Alcaeus exhibits the values and attitudes of the conservative aristocrats of his generation. The center of his existence is a group of noble comrades, probably kinsmen. In times of war, they constitute a unit in the Mytilenaean army. Otherwise, they drink together and conspire to preserve their power and independence. They pride themselves on courage and loyalty, but display little interest in broader issues.

Papyrus Fragments

Oxyrhynchus papyri have yielded eight important fragments of Alcaeus' poems. Oxyrhynchus papyrus 1789 (1st cent. A.D.) contains seven intelligible lines from the end of a poem. Words still legible in earlier lines overlap with a quotation from Alcaeus that is preserved by Heraclitus as an example of allegory (see fragment 9). Combining the two sources, the poems reads:

> Another breaker is heading our way,
> bad as the last. We will have to bail
> until we drop. . . .
> [Three lines are lost.]
> . . . .
> Sail at full speed
> into the mighty harbor!
>
> Not one of us goes soft
> or wavers. A great prize is in sight.
> Think of our previous struggle.
> Give proof of your manhood.
>
> We must not disgrace our noble fathers
> beneath the earth by turning coward. [1]

The next fragment is based on the combination of two papyrus scraps with overlapping texts: Oxyrhynchus papyrus 2302 (1st cent. A.D.) with Cologne 2021 (1st cent. A.D.). Among the legends of Troy was the story that Ajax the Lesser (Ajax son of Oileus) raped the priestess Cassandra in the temple of Athena during the sack of Troy. This angered Athena, who proceeded to make it difficult for the Greek warriors to get home safely. Alcaeus apparently compared an enemy to Ajax the Lesser. Attribution of the poem to him is based on the occurrence of the words "son of Hyrrhas" (= Pittacus) among the remnants of the poem's later lines.

> It would have been far better for the Greeks
> if they had killed the cursed man.
> They would have had a calmer
> sea when they rounded Aegae.
>
> But in the temple Priam's child
> clung to Athena's sacred statue,
> goddess of plunder, touching
> its chin. The enemy marched
>
> through the city. . . . They killed
> Deiphobus. Shouts of *oimoi!* rose
> from the wall and cries of children
> filled the Dardanian plain.
>
> Ajax possessed by a murderous rage
> entered pure Athena's temple,
> most terrible goddess of all
> to those who dishonor the gods.
>
> With both of his hands, the Locrian tore
> the virgin away from the holy statue
> and violently used her, despising
> Zeus' warlike daughter. [2]

Oxyrhynchus papyrus 1233 actually consists of numerous scraps of papyrus, of which several contain only two or three letters. Four passages, however, are well enough preserved for continuous translation. Attribution of these fragments to Alcaeus is based on a minute coincidence. Plutarch happens to quote Alcaeus as saying in one of his poems, "Pour myrrh upon my long-suffering head" (*Convivial Questions* 647E). A small, isolated scrap of 1233 preserves the Greek equivalent of " . . . upon my long-s . . . " Papyrologists infer that this is a portion of the Alcaean line quoted by Plutarch, which makes it likely that the scroll contained a collection of Alcaeus' poetry. Since the style of the surviving fragments is compatible with this hypothesis, the attribution is considered certain.

In the first comprehensible portion of 1233, Alcaeus alludes to the myth of Sisyphus, who extended his life by outsmarting Death, but died in the end and spent eternity pushing a boulder up a hill.

Drink up with me, Melanippus! What makes
you think you can cross the coiling Acheron,
then see the sun's clean light
again? Set no grandiose goals!
King Sisyphus, Aeolus' son
and the smartest man alive, hoped
to conquer Death, but he had to cross
the river again, wise as he was,
and Zeus keeps him hard at work
below. [3]

The next comprehensible section contrasts the adulteress Helen
with Achilles' virtuous mother, the nymph Thetis.

Helen, they say that you and your evil
deeds were bitter pain to Priam
once and his sons, when Zeus burned
holy Ilium.

Noble Peleus took a different
kind of woman in marriage, the delicate
virgin Nereus gave him, and all
the gods were invited.

In Chiron's house he loosened the virgin's
robes. Love blossomed between
him and the best of Nereus' daughters.
A year went by.

She bore him a son, the noblest of heroes,
a charioteer renowned for his chestnut horses,
but the Trojans perished for Helen's sake,
they and their city. [4]

This is followed by the remains of an idyllic scene.

Hebrus, most beautiful of rivers,
from Thrace disgorged, you splash past
Aenus town to the violet sea
. . . .

Young girls crowd your banks
. . . of their thighs . . . with soft hands
. . . they are charmed . . . your wondrous water
like a salve. [5]

Finally, we have an invocation of the friendly deities Castor and Polydeuces, who were thought to take the form of what a later age named St. Elmo's fire, an electrical discharge sometimes seen in stormy weather around the prominent points of airplanes and ships.

> Forsaking Pelops' island, graciously
> show yourselves to me, O mighty
> sons of Leda and Zeus, Castor
> and Polydeuces,
>
> who travel the spreading land and sea
> on horses fleet of foot and easily
> rescue men from the chilly grasp
> of death,
>
> who dart to the top of well-girded vessels
> and dance on the rigging, shedding your light,
> bright from afar, on ships overtaken
> by darkness. [6]

Oxyrhynchus papyrus 2165 (2nd cent. A.D.) preserves parts of two poems that Alcaeus seems to have written in exile after Myrsilus and Pittacus ("son of Hyrrhas") combined to defeat his faction. The ostensible purpose of the first fragment is dedicating a temple, but Alcaeus soon digresses. Diogenes Laertius (1.81) lists "The Gut" as one of Alcaeus' pejorative names for Pittacus.

> This magnificent, sunny
> shrine, open to all, and the altars
> of the blessed immortals within
> were built by men of Lesbos,
>
> who entitled Zeus the "Lord of Suppliants,"
> and you, O glorious, Aeolian Hera
> "Bearer of All" and the third,
> Dionysus, who eats raw
>
> flesh, they named "Kemelios."[1] Come,
> O gods, with kind hearts. Hear
> our prayers and save us from present
> hardship and bitter exile.
>
> And let the Fury of others pursue
> the son of Hyrrhas, since once we vowed
> never . . .
> even one of our comrades,

but either to die, wrapping ourselves
in a blanket of dirt, overcome by those
who . . . or else to kill them,
freeing the people from sorrow.

The Gut never so much as considered
those words in his heart, but casually kicking
his oath aside, he now
makes a feast of our city. [7]

The second fragment is merely an exile's lament.

           I lead
the grueling life of a peasant.
O Agesilaidas, I long to hear
the herald summon assembly

or council! But I have been driven
from lands my father and grandfather
clung to throughout their lives
in the midst of these treacherous townsmen.

I became a backwoods wanderer,
an Onymacles,[2] alone with the wolves.
[Five lines are lost.]
Stepping carefully, I live

where once a year one sees
women of Lesbos in trailing
gowns being judged for beauty
and hears their clamorous invocations. [8]

Quotations

Heraclitus (1st cent. A.D.), the scholar who uses Archilochus' frag-
ment 5 to exemplify allegory, gives two examples from Alcaeus and
one from Anacreon (fragment 1):

> We will also find the lyric poet of Mytilene using allegory; for he makes a
> similar comparison of the disorders associated with tyrants to the stormy
> condition of the sea:
>
> > I cannot tell the winds' direction.
> > Breakers unfurl from this side
> > and that; we go wherever
> > our benighted ship is driven,

desperately battling the storm.
Water edges over the masthold;
the sail, long worn thin,
now has gaping holes;

The anchor lines are slack. [9]

From that maritime image, who would not at first think that sailors'
fear of the sea was the subject? But it is not so. Myrsilus is described and
the growing movement for a tyranny over the Mytilenaeans. In another
passage, Alcaeus makes a veiled reference to the things done by him.

Another breaker is heading our way,
bad as the last. We will have to bail
until we drop. [= fragment 1.1-3]

The islander uses the sea abundantly in allegories and likens most of the
evils suffered on account of tyrants to storms at sea.

The Greeks usually mixed their wine with water. In a discussion of
the proper ratio, Athenaeus speaks of Alcaeus' fondness for drinking:

I recall the words of the lyric poet Alcaeus. Somewhere he says:

Pour it one to two. [10]

Some people think that he is not speaking of the proportion of wine to
water, but that being moderate he only drank unmixed wine one or two
cups at a time. Chamaeleon of Pontus has interpreted the statement this
way, being ignorant of Alcaeus' fondness for wine. He is a poet who is
found drinking in every season and situation. In winter,

Zeus sends rain, a great
storm from heaven, and the streams are frozen.
[Two lines are lost.]

Pile up a fire to beat the weather
down and brim our pots with wine
as sweet as honey, after you circle
your temples with a band of fleecy wool.[3] [11]

In summer,

Wet your lungs with wine. The star wheels round
and the difficult season. All is parched and thirsts.[4] [12]

In spring,

> I have felt the onset of spring, season of flowers.

Going on, he says:

> Mix up a krater of honey-sweet soon as you can! [13]

In the midst of disasters,

> Never surrender your spirit to troubles;
> brooding leads nowhere, Bycchis.
> The one excellent cure
> is pass the wine and get drunk. [14]

To celebrate,

> Time to get drunk! to pass
> your limit! Myrsilus is dead. [15]

And he gives this general advice:

> Plant no other tree before the vine! [16]

How then could one so fond of wine be abstemious and call for only one or two cups at a time? As Seleucus says, the poem itself contradicts those who interpret in that way; for it says,

> Why wait for the lamps at day's last inch?
> Let us drink! Go get some grand, colorful cups!
> The son of Zeus and Semele endowed us with wine
> to forget our cares. Pour it one to two,
> full to the top. Let the bowl be surrounded by jostling cups. [17]

In a later discussion of the emotional effects of music, Athenaeus mentions another of Alcaeus' idiosyncrasies.

In ancient times, music was an incitement to courage. Alcaeus, who was musical if anyone ever was, considered manliness more important than poetry, being warlike to a fault. For example, he proudly says:

> The great hall is ablaze
> with bronze; ranks of bright helmets
> cover the ceiling and spill
> white horsehair crests, ornamentation

for masculine heads. Glistening
metal greaves, legs' rampart
against the arrow's force,
hang on the wall on unseen pegs.
Fresh linen corselets
and hollow shields clutter the floor;
here are blades from Chalcis;
here, belts in abundance and tunics.
From the moment we took on this job,
these are things we could not forget. [18]

Perhaps, it would have been more appropriate for his house to be full of
musical instruments.

John Tzetzes (12th cent. A.D.), commenting on Dionysus' titles in the
Alexandra, a proverbially obscure poem by Lycophron (4th/3rd cent.
B.C.), says that Dionysus is sometimes depicted as a bald old man
because

people who are drunk reveal things that should not logically be spoken.
Thus also Alcaeus says:

Wine reveals the interior man. [19]

Sappho of Lesbos

(7th/6th cent. B.C.)

Sappho lived in Mytilene at the same time as Alcaeus. Judging by her poetry, she remained aloof from politics, although she did spend time in exile before the accession of Pittacus. This suggests that she belonged to one of the leading families of Mytilene. In her extant fragments, she mentions a daughter named Cleis (fragments 2, 28, 39) and a troublesome brother (fragment 3). Herodotus (2.134–35) says that the brother was named Charaxus. He sailed to Egypt to sell wine and ended up buying the freedom of a famous prostitute, for which Sappho scolded him in her poems.

Sappho composed choral wedding hymns and solo love songs for and about other women. From antiquity to the present, her love songs have made her the object of censure and, alternately, special pleading. An early example of the latter is the discussion by Maximus of Tyre (fragments 32–40), who likens Sappho's eroticism to that of the Platonic Socrates. Socrates, however, explicitly claimed to have risen above physical love. There is no evidence of any similar claim or effort on Sappho's part.

Sappho portrays herself as part of an elegant circle of women in which love affairs, rivalries, and painful separations occur. Apparently, women enjoyed considerable freedom of association and expression in Archaic Mytilene and no great stigma was attached to female homosexuality. Beyond that, however, virtually nothing is known about the nature of Sappho's circle. Suggestions that she was a teacher in a kind of finishing school or a priestess of a cult are pure speculation.

As an artist, Sappho is the most admired of the lyric poets, and deservedly so. Her most famous poems (fragments 5, 8, 16) are wonderful blends of conceptual simplicity and delicate feeling, humor and pathos. Her talent was appreciated in antiquity: she was known as the "tenth Muse."

Inscription on a Potsherd

One of the earliest fragments of Sappho's poetry consists of a poorly
spelled inscription on a piece of pottery from the third century B.C.,
which may be taken as evidence of the popularity of Sappho's songs
among the general population. The attribution to Sappho is based
on the fact that the several lines are quoted as Sappho's by later
authors (see, for example, fragment 44).

. . . from Crete descend to this your sacred
shrine. The apple grove will please;
the air is sweet with fumes from the altars'
smoldering incense;

a cold stream murmurs within,
dividing the orchard. Roses block
the sun; sleep glides down
from shivering leaves.

The meadow where horses graze has blossomed
and breezes come in soft breaths.
[Two lines are missing.]

Pick flowers for a garland there,
O Cypris, then come and fill our golden
cups in your delicate manner, sweetening
our joys with nectar. [1]

Papyrus Fragments

One of the early papyrus fragments of Sappho's poetry is constituted
from two scraps of a third-century B.C. scroll that made their way into
separate modern collections: the first ten lines are in Copenhagen,
the final three in Milan. Horizontal lines beside the last three lines
indicate that they were accidentally omitted from an earlier part of
the poem. Originally, they may have introduced the first ten lines.
Attribution is based on the reference to Cleis.

When she was young
my mother said
that braids entwined
with a purple ribbon
were very fetching

on any girl
but for hair that was brighter
than a torch's flame
she recommended garlanded
flowers instead.

There is no stylish
turban for you, Cleis.
Where would I get one? [2]

An Oxyrhynchus papyrus of the third century B.C. preserves verses
concerning a wayward brother. Attribution to Sappho is based on the
information that Herodotus transmits about Sappho's relationship
with her brother.

Cypris and Nereid nymphs, grant
my brother a safe arrival here.
Let him achieve all the goals
his heart has set
and make amends for all his past
mistakes, becoming a joy to his friends,
a grief to his foes. . . . [3]

Another third-century Oxyrhynchus papyrus preserves the only
known stichic composition by Sappho. She describes the scene in
Troy as Hector's wife, Andromache, arrives in the city for the first
time. The passage is unlike anything else known to have been written
by Sappho, but her name is written beside the lines on the papyrus
and lines 8 to 10 are quoted as hers by Athenaeus (460D).

The herald, Idaeus, arrived, a speedy messenger.
. . . .
"Hector and his men are bringing the bright-eyed,
elegant Andromache from holy Thebes and the eternally
flowing Placia across the briny sea
in ships laden with golden bracelets, garments
dyed purple and scented, painted trinkets,
countless silver drinking cups, and ivory."
He spoke. His beloved father leapt to his feet.
Word spread to their friends throughout the city.
At once the ladies of Ilium yoked their mules
to smoothly running carriages and all the throng
of maids and matrons crowded aboard,

but Priam's daughters came by themselves. . . .
Unmarried men attached their horses to chariots.
[An unknown number of lines is lost.]
The sweet pipes were joined by the racket of shells
and sherds being clapped together. Maidens raised
their voices in sacred song, whose echo reached
the sky. . . .
[Three lines are lost.]
Frankincense, cassia, and myrrh filled the air;
women advanced in age shouted their blessings;
the men sang a song of shrill beauty,
calling on Paeon of the lyre who strikes from afar
and singing the praise of godlike Hector and Andromache. [4]

An Oxyrhynchus papyrus of the second century B.C. preserves one of Sappho's most famous poems. Her authorship is confirmed by the grammarian Apollonius Dyscolus (2nd cent. A.D.), who quotes lines 3 and 4 as hers.

Some say a formation of horsemen, infantry,
or ships is the loveliest thing on the black
earth, but I maintain it is whatever
a person loves.

It is perfectly easy to make this clear
to everyone. Helen, who far surpassed
the human race in beauty, deserted
her excellent husband

and went sailing off to Troy with never
a thought for her child or her own dear parents.
Love led her astray. . . .
[Three lines are lost.]

. . . reminds me now of Anactoria,
who is far away.

I would rather see her graceful walk
and the fire in her eyes than all the chariots
the Lydians own or their army marching
in heavy armor. [5]

A sixth-century A.D. papyrus preserved in Berlin contains scraps of three different songs. Attribution is based on Sappho's reference to herself and to Atthis, known from several sources to be the name of one of her friends.

(a)

I honestly want to die!
Preparing to leave in tears,
she had much to say, including:
"Ah, Sappho, we have suffered
so much! I hate to leave you!"
I replied with words like these:
"Go and be well. Remember me.
You know how much we cherished you.
If not, I hope you at least
remember . . .
and beautiful things we shared.
Remember when seated beside me
you crowned yourself with many
a wreath of violets and roses;
and cast around your delicate
neck the garlands we made
by weaving blossoms together.

. . . .
. . . you anointed
yourself with kingly myrrh
and lying on soft beds
. . . satisfied your longing
for delicate. . . . [1]

(b)

"Lord," I said, "I swear
by the blessed goddess, life
above ground gives me no pleasure.
I feel an urge to die
and see the dewy lotus
blooming on Acheron's banks."

(c)

. . . she honored you
like a goddess on earth; your
singing, her special delight.

Now she stands out among
the women of Lydia
like the roseate moon at sunset

outshining the stars; its light
covers the sea
and fields full of flowers

bright with dew; the rose,
chervil, and melilot
rich in honey bloom.

She often paces, remembering
gentle Atthis,
and her heart is consumed by longing. [6]

Quotations

In *Rhetoric* Aristotle (4th cent. B.C.) makes the point that orators
should praise what is noble and censure the disgraceful. He uses
feelings of shame to define nobility and its opposite:

> Noble actions are the opposite of those that cause people shame. People
> are ashamed of saying, doing, and even of intending to do disgraceful
> things, as Sappho wrote in response to the speech of Alcaeus:
>
> "I wish to say a certain thing
> but shame prevents me."
> "If you wanted something noble and fair
> instead of brewing evil with your tongue,
> shame would leave your look;
> you would simply state your claim."[2] [7]

In an essay entitled *On composition*, Dionysius of Halicarnassus (1st
cent. B.C.) says that there are three basic types of style. The austere
style, favored by Pindar and Thucydides, makes each word stand out
by juxtaposing words that do not blend and by using asymmetrical
clauses. The smooth style is the opposite, seeking euphony and sym-
metry. Best is the mixed style, exemplified by Homer, Herodotus,
Sophocles, Plato, and others. It seeks a balance between smoothness
and austerity. Dionysius gives examples of the mixed style, and pro-
ceeds.

> I will quote examples of the smooth style too, choosing Sappho among
> poets and Isocrates from the orators. I will begin with the lyric poetess:
>
> Immortal Aphrodite, enthroned in splendor,
> Zeus' cunning child, I pray,
> make me no slave to regrets,
> madam, and sorrows,

but visit me now, if ever before
you heard my voice from far away,
heeded and came, leaving your father's
palace of gold

in a chariot harnessed to sparrows, lovely
and swift, who guided you through the aether
from sky to black earth with their wings
constantly flapping.

They arrived without warning. I saw your heavenly
face smiling at me, O blessed.
You asked what I suffered from this time, why
I was calling again,

and what in my frenzied soul I wanted
the most to happen. "Whom shall I
persuade to take you back, O Sappho?
Who does you wrong?

"Does she run from you now? She will soon pursue.
She accepts no gifts? Soon she will give them.
She is not in love? She will be soon,
however reluctant."

Come to me now again. Free me
from painful emotion. Make the things
my heart craves happen. Be
my comrade-in-arms. [8]

In a short work listing and defining figures of speech, Tryphon (1st cent. B.C.) defines a proverb as

an utterance addressed to someone else originally but repeated by us in turn to someone of similar character, as in Sappho:

Neither the honey nor the bee for me. [9]

In a more elaborate essay, *On style*, Demetrius (1st cent. A.D.) uses Sappho's poetry to illustrate several rhetorical devices, especially those that produce what he calls "charm." First, in discussing elevated style, he says that the rhetorical figure of *epiphoneme* (additional ornamentation) can contribute a good deal:

One function of language is to convey meaning; another is to embellish it. The following conveys meaning:

> She was like
> a hillside hyacinth the herdsmen trample,

This adds ornamentation:

> and the purple blossom lies on the ground. [10]

These lines are attributed to Sappho on stylistic grounds.

Demetrius contrasts the elevated style with the elegant. Charm, Sappho's forte, is characteristic of the latter:

> Instances of charm produced by figures of speech are clear and frequent in Sappho, e.g., *anadiplosis* [doubling], where a bride says to virginity:

> Maidenhood, maidenhood, where did you go when you left me?

And virginity replies with the same figure:

> To you I shall never return, never return. [11]

Demetrius says that the original purpose of doubling was forcefulness but that Sappho uses it to produce charm. Furthermore, he says,

> she even applies her light touch to *anaphora* [repetition], as in her address to the evening star. "Hesperus," she says, "you bring all things."

> You bring the lamb, you bring the goat,
> you bring the child to its mother. [12]

Later we learn that charm may be produced by comparison; for example,

> Sappho says of an eminent man that he

> stood out like a Lesbian poet abroad. [13]

Moreover,

> there is a peculiarly Sapphic charm produced by variation, when she says one thing and then changes it, as if repenting her initial utterance, as when she says:

 Raise the roofbeam high, O carpenters!

The groom approaches, equal of Ares—
bigger by far than a big man.[3] [14]

It is as though she checked herself because she was using impossible hyperbole: no one is the equal of Ares.

Finally, hyperbolic comparisons can be charming:

Examples are such expressions as *juicier than a melon, balder than clear skies,* and Sappho's verses:

More musical far than a harp,
more golden than gold. [15]

Of the essays on literary criticism that have survived from antiquity, *On the sublime* (1st cent. A.D.) is second only to Aristotle's *Poetics* in the frequency of its quotation by others. Though the author of *On the sublime* is unknown, his name is traditionally given as "Longinus." The essay preserves one of Sappho's most famous poems as part of a discussion of the artful selection of detail in narrative:

In every topic, there is a complex group of elements that is essential to the raw material. Naturally, one cause of sublimity is the consistent selection of the most important of these elements and the ability to arrange them into an organic whole. One author will be admired for his selection of details; another, for his arrangement. In describing erotic passion, Sappho always uses the feelings that result from it in real life. What is her virtue? She is extremely skillful at selecting and combining the most remarkable and intense of these feelings.

To me the man who happens to sit
opposite you seems like a god
as bending close he listens and replies
to your sweet voice

and fetching laughter; such exchange
makes my heart pound with alarm.
Let me so much as glimpse you, my voice
fails me completely.

My tongue is broken; a subtle flame
instantly courses beneath my skin.
No vision is left in my eyes. A whirring
fills my ears.

> Cold sweat flows. Trembling
> shakes my entire frame. I grow
> paler than grass and feel as though
> I have nearly died. [16]

From Hephaestion's *Handbook:*

To what shall I fairly compare you, dear groom?
You seem most like a slender young branch. [17]

The doorman's feet are seven fathoms
Long; making his sandals took
five ox-hides and ten cobblers.[4] [18]

Once I loved you, Atthis, long ago.[5] [19]

Eros leaves me limp and reeling,
that bittersweet, implacable serpent. [20]

Atthis, you hated the very thought
of me. And now you fly to Andromeda! [21]

Pretty Adonis is dying, Cythera. What should we do?
Beat your breasts, maidens, and tear your gowns! [22]

I cannot weave, sweet mother, when I am swooning
with desire for a boy. Blame gentle Aphrodite. [23]

A full moon was shining
as they stood around the altar. [24]

Mnasidica, whose figure surpasses gentle Gyrinno. . . . [25]

Never have you been a greater annoyance, Irana. [26]

Midnight. The moon and Pleiades have set.
Time is passing. I lie alone.[6] [27]

I have a beautiful child, lovely
as flowers of gold, beloved Cleis,
worth more to me than all of Lydia. [28]

O happy groom, the wedding you prayed for
is done; you have the girl of your prayers. [29]

Early in his work, Athenaeus remarks that keeping one's garments properly folded was an important social grace in antiquity. He says that Plato speaks disparagingly of men who did not know how to throw their robes over their right shoulders. Furthermore,

Sappho speaks satirically about Andromeda:

> What peasant girl enchants you,
> wearing a peasant dress
> and lacking the grace to keep her ankles covered? [30]

Later he touches on the question of why people wore floral wreaths while drinking. According to Aeschylus, they were worn in memory of Prometheus' chains, but

Sappho gives a simpler explanation for wearing wreaths in these words:

> Crown your locks with lovely garlands, Dica,
> link shoots of anise with your hands' finesse.
> The blessed Graces are drawn to wherever flowers
> abound, but turn their backs on girls who go wreathless. [31]

Maximus of Tyre (2nd cent. A.D.) was an itinerant lecturer and avid admirer of Plato and Socrates. In one of his lectures, he maintains that Sappho was a kind of female Socrates, with her young favorites and rival teachers:

> She scolds and debates and uses the same kind of irony as Socrates. For example, Socrates says, "I wish you well, Ion," and Sappho says, "I hope that all is well with the daughter of Polyanax." [32] Though Socrates loved Alcibiades greatly, he said that he would not accept his friendship until he was trained in discourse. Sappho says, "You seemed a small and graceless child." [33] Somewhere he ridicules the bearing and table manners of a sophist. She says, "What peasant girl enchants you?" [= 30.1] Diotima tells Socrates that Eros is not the child but the attendant and servant of Aphrodite. Aphrodite says to Sappho in one of her songs, "you and my servant, Eros." [34] Diotima says that Eros blossoms when he has resources but dies without them. Capturing the same idea, Sappho called him "bittersweet" [35; cp. 20] and "pain-giving." [36] Socrates calls Eros a sophist; Sappho, "story-weaver." [37] Socrates feels "Dionysiac madness" because of his love for Phaedrus; for Sappho, "love shakes my mind, like the wind on mountain oaks." [38] Socrates criticizes Xanthippe for lament-

ing his death. Sappho rebukes her daughter: "Mourning is not the custom in the house of the Muses' servants and would ill become us." [39]

Stobaeus preserves two passages:

> You will soon be dead and buried and no one will ever
> mention you again, because you disdain the roses
> of Pierian song. Flown from here you will wander
> with corpses in twilight, unnoticed even in Hell.[7] [40]

> I know you love me, but marry a younger woman;
> I will not play the part of an older wife. [41]

A fifth-century A.D. commentator on Hermogenes lists topics that are conducive to stylistic "sweetness." Among them are sensually pleasing descriptions;

for example Sappho:

> a cold stream murmurs within dividing the orchard [= 2.5–6]

and

> as a sweet apple blushes on the tree's
> highest branch. Overlooked by the pickers?
> No. They could not reach that high. [42]

Eustathius (12th cent. A.D.) commenting on *Iliad* 8.555, in which Homer compares the Trojan camp fires to the stars that surround the shining moon, cautions that

one should not think here of the light of the full moon. In that case, stars are dim because of being outshone, as Sappho says somewhere:

> Stars put their beauty back
> in hiding when the lovely moon approaches
> and shines in fullness upon the earth. [43]

Stesichorus of Himera

(7th/6th cent. B.C.)

All the authors of fragments translated so far lived either in the Aegean region or on mainland Greece. Poetry was also being composed by Greeks in Sicily and southern Italy. The two early western poets from whose works we have meaningful fragments flourished shortly after Sappho. One was Stesichorus. The *Suda* gives his birthplace as Mataurus in southern Italy or Himera on the north coast of Sicily, and his dates as 632/629 to 556/553. The dates are generally accepted; perhaps he was born in the small town of Mataurus, but worked in Himera.

The *Suda* also states that Stesichorus wrote twenty-six books of poetry. Very few fragments of his verse survive, however, and Campbell has suggested that his output may actually have consisted of just twenty-six poems.[1]

In his poems, whatever their number, Stesichorus recast myths and legends as choral songs. The story was told that he lost his sight after reciting a poem about Helen's infidelity and regained it when he rewrote the story in a way that salvaged her reputation. The revisionist work, known as the *Palinode* (*Recantation*), asserted that the Greeks and Trojans fought over a phantom, while the real Helen sojourned chastely in Egypt. The beginning of the poem is preserved by Plato.

Though Stesichorus was influential in his day, there is little that is memorable in the verses that do survive. As the story of Helen suggests, his genius lay in embellishing the plots of traditional tales. His two longest fragments (1 and 2) are preserved on papyrus; in both cases, attribution is based chiefly on stylistic grounds and is probable but not certain. Both are excerpts from narratives; fragment 1 concerns the sons of Oedipus, while fragment 2 describes the slaying of a giant. The latter is probably from Stesichorus' *Geryoneis*, the

tale of Heracles' tenth labor. This was to steal the cattle of the three-
bodied Geryon, who inhabited an island in the far west on the shore
of Oceanus. To get there, Heracles borrowed the golden cup in which
the Sun sails east at night (fragment 6). The tale had special signifi-
cance for Himerans. Their city was a recently founded colony on
Sicily's northwest coast, located there in order to make trade with
Spain easier.

Papyrus Fragments

The longest fragment attributed to Stesichorus was discovered in
1974, among the wrappings of a mummy of the second century B.C.
that was stored at the University of Lille. The fragment comes from
a poem about the sons of Oedipus, Eteocles and Polyneices, who
killed each other fighting over the Theban throne. In the preserved
excerpt, their mother, Jocasta, tries to prevent their fatal conflict,
which the prophet Tiresias has evidently just predicted.

*peace-
maker*

"To present pain refrain from adding
dire prospect;
silence your burdensome prophecies!

The immortal gods
have not ordained that strife should last
forever on holy earth,
or love for that matter. Day by day they change
the hearts of men.
May Lord Apollo, who strikes from afar, not
fulfill your oracles.

But if I am destined to see my sons slain
by each other and the Fates have woven it so,
may death, however hateful, take me now,
before I view
such a scene of lamentation and pain:
my boys lying dead
in the palace or the city fallen.

Come, dear sons, heed my words.
It is I who reveal the ending now:
one of you keep the palace and dwell in Cadmeia;
the other, the one
whose lot is first to be drawn, leave,

but take your possessions
and all your father's gold.

That way I think
frees you from evil fate, according
to our holy prophet's revelations,
if Zeus will preserve this new generation and city
of Cadmus by delaying
a length of time the disaster destined to crush
our royal family."

So spoke the noble lady, urging her sons
with gentle words to end their quarrel. [1]

An Oxyrhynchus papyrus of the 1st century A.D. preserves what may
be Stesichorus' description of the death of Geryon.

. . . Still as a thief,
he took aim at the forehead.
As a god decreed, he parted flesh
and bones.
Straight from the top of Geryon's skull
the shaft protruded.
Blood left its scarlet stain
on chest and reeking arms and legs.
Then Geryon's neck slackened and fell,
like a fragile stalk that breaks
beneath the weight of a poppy's blossom.
Soon the leaves wither.[2] [2]

Quotations

In the *Phaedrus*, Plato (5th/4th cent. B.C.) depicts Socrates as suddenly
regretting the fact that Eros, a divinity, has been referred to as evil
in the course of the conversation.

Now I must be purified, friend. There is an ancient form of purification
for those sinning in mythological matters. Homer was not aware of it, but
Stesichorus was. He was deprived of his eyesight because he spoke ill of
Helen. Unlike Homer, he knew the cause, being a scholar, and immedi-
ately composed the lines: ~~died~~, regfound sight

The story is false.
You never boarded the sturdy ships
or came to Troy's towers. [3]

And when he finished his entire palinode, as it is called, his sight was restored.

In an essay attempting to explain the "Slowness of Divine Vengeance," Plutarch argues that all sinners suffer the internal pains of a guilty conscience, including nightmares. Hence,

> Stesichorus modeled the dream of Clytemnestra on reality and truth when he said:
>
>> She dreamt a serpent approached, head bloodied;
>> from which a Pleisthenid king appeared."[3] [4]

Athenaeus does not fail to discuss different types of fruit. He maintains that those with the most juice are least digestible. Among winter apples, quinces produce more astringent juices, those called *strouthia* less. Furthermore,

> Stesichorus mentions quinces in his poem "Helen" in the following lines:
>
>> As the chariot passed, they pelted their king with quince apples,
>> a flood of myrtle leaves,
>> rosy garlands and violet-thick wreaths. [5]

Evidently, this describes the ill-starred wedding of Helen and Menelaus.

Athenaeus' catalog of drinking vessels includes a discussion of the golden cup in which the Sun sailed on Oceanus (see also Mimnermus fragment 1) and which Heracles borrowed or stole for his journey to Geryon's kingdom. Judging by Athenaeus' citation, Stesichorus' *Geryoneis* included this motif with the peculiarity that Helios used the cup to finish his own westward journey, not to return east:

> Stesichorus informs us that Helios was also conveyed towards the west in the cup in these words:
>
>> Helios, son of Hyperion, sank down in the cup
>> of gold, wherein he would travel across Oceanus
>> to the innermost reaches of Night's holy gloom,
>> to his mother, wedded wife, and children dear, while Zeus'
>> son continued on foot to a wood
>> dark with laurels. [6]

In Euripides' *Orestes*, the hero says that King Tyndareus was unlucky in his daughters, Clytemnestra and Helen. A scholiast remarks,

Stesichorus says that Tyndareus was sacrificing to the gods once when he forgot to include Aphrodite. In her anger, the goddess made his daughters marry two and three times and abandon their husbands. He phrases it this way:

One day Tyndareus
made sacrifice to all the gods but absentmindedly
omitted gentle Aphrodite. Furious,
she made his daughters marry two times and three
and desert their husbands. [7]

Ibycus of Rhegium

(6th cent. B.C.)

The other native westerner for us to consider is Ibycus, who flour-
ished in the 530s. He was born in Rhegium, on the toe of Italy. He is
most admired for the deft imagery contained in a couple of erotic
fragments (4 and 5).

After making a name for himself, Ibycus came east and took up
residence in the court of Polycrates, the colorful tyrant of Samos.
Polycrates was one of the dominant personalities of the Greek world
from approximately 535, when he seized control of Samos, to ap-
proximately 522, when he was murdered by a Persian governor.

Papyrus Fragment

Fragment 1 is attributed to Ibycus chiefly because of the flattering
reference it contains to Polycrates, whom it compares to the heroes
of the Trojan War. The Polycrates involved may have been the ty-
rant's son, Polycrates junior. The fragment is preserved on an
Oxyrhynchus papyrus that is said to be datable to approximately 130
B.C. It is not known how much of the poem is lost.

Rising from Argos they sacked Dardanian	ant.
Priam's great and famous city,	
prosperous once,	
as Zeus the great decreed.	
Many have sung the strife	ep.
they endured in tearful combat	
for the beauty of blonde-haired Helen	
and destruction arrived at sorrowful Pergamum	
through Cypris whose hair is like gold;	9
but my heart is not now set upon singing	st.
of Paris who tricked his host, of Cassandra's	

slender ankles,
or Priam's other children,

or the unspeakable day the enemy captured
Troy despite its lofty gates,
nor will I recount
the eminent virtue of heroes

brought for Troy's destruction   ep.
in the holds of sturdy ships,
mighty Agamemnon's troop,   20
Pleisthenid king, leader of men,
and son of noble Atreus.

Mount Helicon's masterful Muses   st.
might well embark on such a tale;
no mortal living
could give a complete account

of all the ships that departed Aulis,   ant.
crossed the Aegean sea from Greece,
and came to Troy,
the nurse of horses, or the men   30

on board, the sons of Achaea with brazen   ep.
shields. Noblest in battle
were Achilles, fleet of foot,
valiant Telamonian Ajax the great,
[Six lines are lost.]

. . . the son of Hyllis wrapped   ant.
in gold. So beautiful was his form,   41
the Trojans and Greeks
compared him to Troilus, as if

comparing gold refined   ep.
three times to brass.
They will always have their share
of beauty, and you, Polycrates, of fame,
lasting as the fame of my song. [1]

*flattering
patron*

Quotations

In a wide-ranging essay called *Convivial Questions*, Plutarch says that
the art of dancing has degenerated in his time:

These days nothing has been nourished by bad taste more than dancing.
In fact, it has experienced what Ibycus wrote about:

> I fear gaining honor from men
> by giving offense to the gods. [2]

When the conversation turns to eggs, Athenaeus adduces several strange tales and an excerpt from Ibycus' poetry. The sons of Molione were obscure heroes eventually killed by Heracles. No other source confirms what Ibycus says about them.

> Neocles of Croton was mistaken in saying that the egg from which Helen was born fell from the moon. As Herodorus of Heracleia reports, moon-women lay eggs but their offspring are fifteen times larger than we are. In the fifth book of his songs, Ibycus says:

> > I killed the lads on white
> > horses, sons of Molione,
> > alike in age and face, sharing one body,
> > and both of them born in a silver egg.[1] [3]

In the passage in which he credits Alcman with inventing love songs, Athenaeus gives other examples of the genre.

> Ibycus of Rhegium cries out:

> > Only in spring, when they drink
> > from flowing rivers, do quince
> > trees bloom in the maidens' — nymphs
> > inviolate garden, and budding blossoms
> > start to swell in the leafy shade
> > of the vine, but there is no season
> > when Eros sleeps for me.
> > He swoops from Cypris' side
> > like a freezing Thracian wind
> > that comes with thunder and lightning, a dark,
> > bold god who throws
> > my mind into utter confusion
> > and scorches it with madness. [4]

In Plato's *Parmenides*, a difficult metaphysical dialogue, the philosopher Parmenides is asked to explain the implications of the hypothesis that the One exists and of the opposite hypothesis, that it does not exist. He reluctantly agrees to do, saying,

> I now think I know how that horse of Ibycus felt. He was a rather old race horse who was about to compete pulling a chariot. He trembled, knowing

from past experience what going to happen. The poet compared himself
to the horse, saying that despite his age he was falling in love against his
will. And I feel myself growing fearful when I think what a sea of words
I will have to swim at my advanced age.

In his commentary on the dialogue, Proclus (5th cent. A.D.) gives us
additional information:

This is what the lyric poet says:

Eros' eyes have stunned me again
with a melting glance from beneath his darkened
lids; he uses every spell
to entangle me in the Cyprian's endless
net. Seeing him approach, I shudder,
like an aging horse, a champion charioteer, yoked
to his speedy car and reluctantly nearing the gate. [5]

Phocylides of Miletus

(6th cent. B.C.)

Ionian poets who reached adulthood about the time of the Persian occupation of their homeland constitute the largest group in this volume. The first of these is the Milesian Phocylides who flourished, according to the *Suda*, in the very years (544/1) that the Persians arrived. Miletus, however, was the one Ionian city that came to terms with the Persian king Cyrus peaceably. It is not known what involvement, if any, Phocylides had in these matters. He wrote maxims in dactylic hexameter, often beginning: *kai tode Phokylidou* (also this [is a saying] of Phocylides). One wry elegiac couplet (fragment 2) is attributed to him. Dio Chrysostom's introduction to fragment 3 shows that Phocylides' terse style and self-advertisement were found amusing even in antiquity.

Quotations

In his *Politics*, Aristotle (4th cent. B.C.) makes the point that members of the middle class have relatively safe lives:

> Unlike the poor, they do not envy the property of others, nor do others envy theirs, as the poor envy the rich. Because they do not lay plots and are not plotted against, their lives are not dangerous. So Phocylides' wish is a good one:
>
> > A middle position has many advantages; it is where
> > I want to be in the city. [1]

Strabo the geographer (1st cent. B.C./1st cent. A.D.) uses an elegiac couplet by Phocylides to enliven a list of Aegean islands.

> There is also Amorgos, one of the Sporades, where Semonides the iambic poet was born, Lebinthos, and Leros:

> Thus spoke Phocylides:
> Lerians are bad, not some, but all, except
> Procles, and Procles is a Lerian.[1] [2]

Men from Leros, you see, were derided for having evil ways.

Dio Chrysostom (1st/2nd cent. A.D.), the traveling orator who pre-
served Archilochus' lines on tall commanders (fragment 6), also tells
a story involving Phocylides. He was visiting the rough city of
Borysthenes on the shore of the Black Sea, where Homer and his
Achilles were idolized. Conversing with a prominent local youth, he
asked him facetiously whether he considered Homer or Phocylides
the better poet. The youth had never heard of Phocylides; so Dio
began to praise him:

> His poems have a beginning and an end in two or three verses. He at-
> taches his name to each sentiment, because he considers it important and
> valuable, whereas Homer never refers to himself by name. But doesn't it
> seem appropriate for Phocylides to attach himself to a sentiment like this:
>
> > Thus spoke Phocylides: a little mountain town
> > well-governed is stronger than mindless Nineveh. [3]
>
> Do these words not seem uplifting for people who listen attentively, even
> if they are compared with the entire *Iliad* and *Odyssey*?

Stobaeus preserves four fragments of Phocylides' work:

> Many men whose minds are far from stable
> seem to be wise because of their dignified carriage. [4]

> If you long for wealth, tend a fertile farm.
> A farm, they say, is Amalthea's horn of plenty. [5]

> Thus spoke Phocylides. These are the four sources
> of women: they descend from the dog, the bee, the bristling
> boar, and the long-maned mare. The child of the mare
> is graceful, fleet, attractive, and runs around;
> the boar's descendant is neither good nor bad;
> the dog's is difficult and crude, but the bee's is good
> at keeping an orderly house and knows how to work.
> Pray for a happy marriage to her, my friend. [6]

Thus spoke Phocylides. What good is noble birth
in men whose words and counsel are void of grace? [7]

The *Anthology* of Orion of Thebes (5th cent. A.D.) attributes these
lines to Phocylides:

Lay your plans by night. At night the mind
is sharper and quiet is good for seeking virtue. [8]

A scholiast commenting on Aristophanes' play *Clouds* remarks that
the playwright's word for creditors (*chresteis*) means *debtors* in other
authors. For example,

Phocylides following normal usage calls debtors *chresteis*, saying:

Avoid becoming a scoundrel's
debtor. He makes untimely demands for repayment. [9]

Hipponax of Ephesus

(6th cent. B.C.)

Hipponax, a master of abuse, flourished 540–537 and was a native of Ephesus, but he was banished by the tyrants who governed the city on behalf of the Persians and went to live in nearby Clazomenae. He was particularly remembered for attacks against two sculptors, Bupalus and Athenis. Pliny the Elder (*Natural History* 36.11) provides some of the details:

> [Hipponax'] face was remarkably ugly. Hence [Bupalus and Athenis] displayed a mischievously amusing likeness of him to laughing audiences. Infuriated, Hipponax wrote such bitter poems that one of them supposedly drove the sculptors to suicide by hanging. But that is untrue; for they later erected numerous statues on neighboring islands, for example, on Delos.

Hipponax was credited with the invention of "choliambic" or "limping iambic" verse: this is an iambic line that ends with a spondee in the last foot, and thus creates a stumbling rhythm. A few mutilated fragments (e.g., 1) imply that he composed fairly extensive narratives set among the dregs of his contemporary society. If more had survived, he might have displaced Petronius as the chief ancient forerunner of modern comic novelists.

Papyrus Fragments

A second-century A.D. papyrus preserves the longest extant segment of Hipponax' comic narrative. Attribution is based on the citation of lines 10 and 11 in later authors.

She spoke in Lydian . . .
indecently, "The buttocks . . .

and testicles for me. . . ."
She beat me with twigs . . .
. . . with forked branch . . .
in two kinds of trouble. . . .
A twig on either side. . . .
She attacked from above. . . .
Dripping with excrement. . . .
The latrine was rank. Over five hundred
dung beetles were drawn by the odor.
Some attacking . . .
cast down, others. . . .[1] [1]

Another second-century papyrus preserves a magnificent expression of hatred. Attribution to Hipponax is based on the occurrence of his name among the mutilated remains of another poem originally appearing on the same page.

I hope he is lost at sea
and a band of Thracian topknots gleefully
catches him, naked at Salmydessus,
and there he runs the gamut of sorrow
eating slaves' bread.
Frozen stiff, covered with seaweed
and foam, teeth chattering,
lying flat on his face in the surf
like a dog . . .
that is how I wish to see
the man who wronged me, trampling oaths,
and used to be my friend. [2]

Quotations

The lexicographer Erotian (1st cent. A.D.) says that poets use the word *amphidexios* (ambidextrous) of swords that are sharp on both sides, while the physician Hippocrates applies it to facility with limbs on both sides of the body.

Similarly, Hipponax says:

I am an ambidexter; my punches never miss. [3]

From Hephaestion's *Handbook:*

I wish I had a virgin, delicate and fair! [4]

We learn from Athenaeus that tuna fish was often mentioned as a delicacy by poets:

As quoted by Lysanias in his works on iambic poets, Hipponax says:

Creeping off to feast every day on tuna
and cheese reeking with honey and garlic,
he dined like a Lampsacene eunuch until
not a crumb was left—of his inheritance.
Now he hoes a rocky hillside, eating
mediocre figs and barley, slave-fodder. [5]

Later Athenaeus makes the interesting claim that Hipponax invented parody. Although Euboeus of Paros (4th cent. B.C.) was the most famous author of parodies, he says,

credit for discovering the genre should go to the iambic poet Hipponax. In his hexameter verses, he says:

Sing of the son of Eurymedon, Muse! He could drain
the sea, old "Knives-in-the-Belly," a disgusting glutton.
And tell of his wretched forthcoming death: stoning
by public decree on the shore of the barren sea. [6]

Stobaeus preserves one fragment:

A woman pleases twice, on the day
she weds and the day they remove her corpse. [7]

The *Suda* (10th cent. A.D.) quotes two lines under the proper name Bupalus. Apparently, Hipponax's abuse of the sculptor had made his name proverbial.

Aristophanes writes, "If by Zeus someone hit their jaws two or three times, like Bupalus', they couldn't speak." Also in Hipponax:

Hold my cloak while I punch Bupalus in the eye. [8]

The *Chiliades* by John Tzetzes (12th cent. A.D.) is a poetic commentary on the author's own letters, which are full of learned allusions. The

title, meaning "Thousands," refers to the length of the work, 12,674
lines. In one interesting passage, Tzetzes quotes lines from Hipponax
in explaining his own use of the word *pharmakos* (scapegoat). Use of
the *pharmakos* was a savage ritual allegedly practiced by Greek city-
states in times of stress. It is not known how accurate Tzetzes' ac-
count is. He may have made unjustified historical inferences from
literary sources.

The *pharmakos* was an ancient rite of purification:
if by wrath of god disaster struck a city,
be it plague, famine, or other distress,
the people led their ugliest man to sacrifice
as a means of cleansing and curing the suffering city.
They took the victim to a spot that fit the occasion,
gave him cheese, a barley loaf, and figs;
then flogged him, hitting his privates seven times
with dried wild onions and other weeds.
They burned him at last on a pyre of wild timber
and sprinkled his ashes abroad to the sea and winds,
a means, as I said, of cleansing the suffering city.
But Hipponax describes the entire custom best:

To cleanse the city and be beaten by branches. [9]

Elsewhere in his first volume of iambs he writes:

Attacked in the meadow and flogged him with twigs
and wild onions as if a *pharmakos*. [10]

And again in other places he says, to quote:

We must choose him to be our *pharmakos*. [11]

To place dry figs and barley bread
in hand and the cheese that *pharmakoi* eat. [12]

They have anxiously waited for some time now,
holding the branches they use on *pharmakoi*. [13]

Elsewhere in the same volume of iambs he says:

May he be led like a *pharmakos*, withered
by hunger and struck seven times in the manhood. [14]

Tzetzes also cites Hipponax in his commentary on Lycophron's *Alexandra*. Once he is merely illustrating a metrical point. Both authors treat the initial syllable in *ophis* (snake) as a long, even though an aspirated consonant like *ph* does not normally close a syllable. The relevant lines by Hipponax are addressed to a ship-painter.

> Mimnes, you gaping ass, never
> paint the snake on a trireme's side
> running from prow to pilot in back!
> Think what a disaster and omen,
> O filthy slave from birth, if a snake
> should happen to bite the pilot's shin! [15]

Later he takes Lycophron to task for using the word *askerai* as if it meant "sandals." Tzetzes says Lycophron borrowed the word from Hipponax but failed to notice that it refers to warm felt boots.

Hear how Hipponax speaks and learn that *askerai* are not sandals but felt boots. Hipponax says:

> You never gave me a shaggy cloak,
> Remedy for winter's cold,
> Or wrapped my feet in shaggy boots [*askerai*]
> To prevent attacks of frostbite. [16]

Do you need further evidence? Listen:

> Beloved Hermes, Maia's son,
> Cyllene's lord. . . .

After these words he says:

> Give Hipponax a cloak, a wispy
> tunic, slippers, bootees [*askeriska*], and sixty
> pieces of gold from the other side. [17]

In Aristophanes' *Plutus* (*Wealth*), the god of wealth is described as being blind. A scholiast comments,

Aristophanes borrows the idea of calling Wealth blind from Hipponax. For Hipponax says:

Wealth, you *must* be totally blind!
Not once have you come to my house saying,
"Thirty pieces of silver for Hipponax
and more!" You have a defective intellect. [18]

hubs.

Xenophanes of Colophon

(6th century B.C.)

Xenophanes was a younger contemporary of Hipponax. He was born in wealthy Colophon, which surrendered to the Persians in 540. His description of a symposium (fragment 4) exemplifies Ionian luxuriousness. He himself informs us (fragment 15) that he left home at the age of twenty-five and spent the next sixty-seven years traveling around the Greek world. It is generally assumed that he began traveling because of the Persian conquest and his dates are based on this assumption. In fragment 2, Xenophanes recommends the question "How old were you when the Mede came?" as a good way to start a conversation. This supports the conjecture that the invasion marked a turning point in his own life.

Apparently, Xenophanes' travels took him west: his ancient biographer, Diogenes Laertius, says that he lived in Zancle and Catane in Sicily and Aristotle mentions that that philosopher Parmenides of Elea (in southern Italy) was his pupil. Aristotle's assertion, however, may be only an inference based on the resemblance of Parmenides' philosophy to Xenophanes'.

Indeed, Xenophanes' verse occupies the border between poetry and philosophy. He deals with philosophical topics, but does so in a humorous and concrete manner. One of his works was entitled *Silloi* (*Lampoons*); another, mentioned in fragment 2, *Parodies*. He is best known for his criticism of the theology of Homer and Hesiod. Although he sometimes speaks as though he believes in the traditional gods (fragment 4.24), in more philosophical moments he rejects anthropomorphic polytheism altogether and describes a single transcendent divinity (fragments 7–12, 17–19).

Quotations

In a list of irregular words, Herodian the grammarian (2nd cent. A.D.) says that adjectives with upsilon (υ) in their roots do not have comparative forms ending in *-on*, but that Xenophanes' word for sweeter (*glysson*) in the following lines is an exception:

> If god had not created yellow honey,
> people would say that figs were quite a bit sweeter. [1]

Athenaeus preserves four substantial fragments of Xenophanes' work. First, in a catalog of fruits, berries, and nuts, he adduces verses of Xenophanes because they contain a reference to chickpeas.

> Lying on a comfortable couch by a fire
> in winter, full, sipping sweet
> wine and nibbling chickpeas say:
> "Your name? Your people? Your years, good sir?
> How old were you when the Mede came?" [2]

On the topic of gluttony, Athenaeus says that athletes are particularly prone to this fault and quotes a famous criticism of athletes by Euripides.[1] He adds that

> Euripides took his ideas from the elegies of Xenophanes of Colophon, who said:

> > Suppose a man is first in speed of foot
> >   or pentathlon at Zeus' precinct
> > in Olympia where Pisa flows, or wins at wrestling,
> >   the painful art of boxing,
> > or the fearsome sport called pancratium; his townsmen
> >   think him a glorious sight.
> > The city awards him a seat of honor at games,
> >   food at public expense,
> > a gift to keep as an heirloom. A man whose horses
> >   win is treated the same,
> > but he is not my equal. My wisdom is better
> >   than strength of men or horses.
> > Custom is wrong; it is not just to honor
> >   strength ahead of wisdom.

Being good as a boxer, in pentathlon, or wrestling
 gives nothing to the people;
no city ever becomes better governed
 by speed of foot, the most
valued kind of strength in all athletics.
 Small is the city's benefit
when a man wins a prize on the banks of Pisa;
 no storage rooms are fatter. [3]

Though it is seldom obvious, Athenaeus' work is cast as a conversation among erudite men at a banquet. At one point, one of them remarks that their banquet is

full of everything that gives pleasure, just as Xenophanes of Colophon said:

The floor and everyone's hands and cups are clean.
 A boy distributes garlands,
another fills a bowl with perfumed oil.
 The krater is full of cheer
and the wine in reserve, sweet of bouquet and taste,
 boasts it will never run out.
The holy odor of incense spreads; cold
 is the water, and sweet and pure.
There are golden loaves and the stately table groans
 beneath cheese and honey.
The central altar is thick with flowers; music
 and celebration embrace the house.
Right-thinking men must first hymn god
 with reverent tales, then pour
libations and pray to be able to do what is just,
 for that is more beneficial.
Your drinking is not excessive, if you get home
 unaided—unless you are aged.
Praise him who reveals nobility drinking, sound
 memory, and devotion to virtue.
He does not recount battles of Titans, Giants
 or Centaurs, our ancestors' inventions,
or civil violence: tales without profit. Respect
 for the gods is always in order. [4]

On the topic of luxury, Athenaeus says that many cities have fallen because of it. For example,

Phylarchus says that the people of Colophon were austere in their manners at first, but they drifted into luxury after becoming the friends and allies of the Lydians. Then they went around with golden ornaments in their hair. Xenophanes also says this:

> They were students of vain Lydian luxury until
>   they succumbed to hated despotism.
> A thousand, no fewer, would go to assembly
>   in cloaks of solid purple,
> boastful, priding themselves on their hair's appearance,
>   and steeped in exotic scents. [5]

The skeptical philosopher Sextus Empiricus (3rd cent. A.D.) cites Xenophanes on several occasions. In one passage, he mentions the theory that there simply is no criterion by which truth can be identified.

According to some, Xenophanes is of this inclination, having declared all things incomprehensible in this passage:

> Concerning the gods and whatever I say about anything,
> no one has any certainty, nor ever will;
> and if someone should happen to utter the absolute truth,
> how would he know it? Seeming is present in everything. [6]

Elsewhere Sextus uses a line from Xenophanes' description of god as part of a proof that a divine being could not exist. The line is attributed to Xenophanes because of a paraphrase of it in Diogenes Laertius' life of Xenophanes. Sextus says,

If the divine exists, it is animate. If it is animate, it sees.

With all of his being, He sees and thinks and hears. [7]

The rest of the argument is that sense perception implies change in the perceiver. What can change can perish. The divine cannot perish. Therefore it does not exist.

In arguing against the existence of the gods, Sextus mentions the impiety of their depiction in mythology and poetry, adding that

in disputing the followers of Homer and Hesiod, Xenophanes says:

Homer and Hesiod sully the gods
with every form of shame and disgrace:
stealing, adultery, and mutual deception. [8]

The Christian theologian Clement of Alexandria (3rd cent. A.D.) cites Xenophanes' view of god's nature sympathetically. Like Christians,

Xenophanes of Colophon teaches that god is one and bodiless:

God is one, the greatest of gods and men
resembling mortals neither in body or mind. [9]

Again:

But mortals think that gods are born,
wear clothes, have bodies and voices. [10]

And again:

If cows and horses or lions had hands
and made works of art like men,
the horses' gods would look like horses,
the cows' like cows; and they would model
the bodies of the gods upon their own. [11]

Clement especially likes Xenophanes' criticism of Greek anthropomorphism.

The Greeks assume that the gods have human feelings as well as human form, and just as each race depicts the gods' forms as resembling itself, as Xenophanes says:

The gods of Ethiopia are black, their noses flat;
in Thrace, their hair is red and eyes are blue. [12]

In the same way, they consider their souls similar and represent them as having the same feelings.

Diogenes Laertius (3rd cent. A.D.) quotes Xenophanes in his life of Pythagoras to exemplify the criticism that Pythagoras incurred because of his solemnity and his belief in reincarnation.

Xenophanes bears witness to Pythagoras' claim that he had been a differ-
ent person at a different time in the elegy beginning:

I come to a different tale and will show the way. [13]

antiqu. What he says about [reincarnation] goes:

    They say he passed a man beating a puppy,
        pitied and uttered this speech:
    "Stop! Don't strike! He is a dear friend's
        soul. I recognize the bark." [14]

In his brief life of Xenophanes, Diogenes only quotes Xenophanes
directly to establish his longevity:

Xenophanes was very long-lived as he himself says somewhere:

    The years are sixty-seven now that have tossed
        my thoughts around Greece;
    from birth twenty-five preceded my travels, if I know
        how to count them accurately. [15]

Stobaeus preserves one fragment of Xenophanes:

    The gods did not reveal all things at once
    to mortals; by long investigation understanding grows. [16]

Commenting on Aristotle's *Physics,* Simplicius (6th cent. A.D.) says
that, according to Xenophanes, god transcends such distinctions as
finite or infinite, moving or at rest.

Even when he says that god stays in the same place without moving,

    He always remains in the same place, motionless;
    it is not fitting for him to chase now here, now there, [17]

he is not speaking of the rest that is the opposite of motion but of perma-
nence removed from both motion and rest.

Later we learn that Xenophanes' god is a disembodied intellect, for

[Xenophanes] also says that [god] apprehends all things:

By effortless thought he controls all things with his mind. [18]

In the *Iliad* (11.27), Homer compares Agamemnon's shield to a rain-
bow, which was customarily personified as the goddess Iris. This
leads a scholiast to remark that

Xenophanes says:

> The lady called Iris is also a cloud,
> purple, red, and yellow to view. [19]

Anacreon of Teos

(6th/5th cent. B.C.)

Anacreon was from Teos, one of two cities (Phocaea being the other) whose inhabitants preferred to emigrate *en masse* rather than submit to Persian rule. The Teans made their way to Thrace, where they founded the city of Abdera. Anacreon participated in this adventure. His poem to a "Thracian filly" (fragment 1) may have been composed at this juncture. Either in Abdera or earlier in Teos he gained recognition as a poet, since he went from Thrace to the court of Polycrates.

There he apparently became one of the most famous poets of his day. When Polycrates was murdered, the rulers of Athens sent a warship to escort Anacreon safely to their court. These rulers were the sons of Pisistratus. Their father had died peaceably in 528/7 after giving Athens two decades of good government. His eldest son, Hippias, succeeded him as tyrant. Hippias' brother, Hipparchus, who took a special interest in cultural matters, was responsible for importing Anacreon.

Later generations viewed Anacreon as the epitome of sophisticated sensuality, and they produced numerous, inferior imitations of his poetry. The loss of the originals is certainly regrettable. As things stand, only a few gems remain to help us understand his fame: his lines on the Thracian filly, a boy with girlish eyes (21), a girl in elaborate sandals (22), and his fear of death (23).

Quotations

Heraclitus (1st cent. A.D.), the author of an essay on Homeric allegory who preserves Archilochus 5 and Alcaeus 8, also quotes an allegorical passage from Anacreon.

In abusing the meretricious character and arrogance of a pompous woman, the Tean Anacreon used the allegory of a horse to describe her uncontrollable temperament.

> Why look down your nose at me, little Thracian filly?
> Why always avoid me? Do you think I have no skill or knowledge?
> Know I could bridle you nicely, take the reins and finish
> the course. You graze in meadows now, frisking free
> of care, because you lack a skillful, experienced rider. [1]

The geographer Strabo (1st cent. B.C./1st cent. A.D.) says that cities on the coast of Spain were always very prosperous.

One may assume that it was from this prosperity that its inhabitants, especially their leaders, are called *macraeones* [long-lived] and that for this reason Anacreon wrote:

> I would not want to own
> Amalthea's horn or spend
> a hundred and fifty years
> as king of Tartessus. [2]

In one of his edifying lectures, Dio Chrysostom says that kings should listen only to virile militaristic music. Furthermore,

a king's prayers should not resemble those of other men. He should not call upon the gods in the manner of the Ionians' poet Anacreon:

> Lord, who revels
> on mountain tops
> with conquering Eros,
> dark-eyed nymphs,
> and blushing Aphrodite,
> I clasp your knee.
> Be kind, hear
> and accept my prayer:
> Counsel Cleobulus
> well; make him
> welcome my love,
> O Dionysus! [3]

From Hephaestion's *Handbook* and "On Poems":

I love and do not love!
I am mad and I am not mad! [4]

Bald Alexis is courting another girl. [5]

I dined on a sliver of fluffy cake and jar
of wine. Now I strum my harp of desire
and sing a sweet song to my dear Poliarche. [6]

Eros worked me over again with a blacksmith's
hammer and doused me in icy water. [7]

Just let me die! No other escape
from troubles like mine is possible. [8]

In flight from Eros, I slipped
away again to Pythomandros. [9]

Tempestuous Ares loves a steady spearman. [10]

Deer-slayer, I beseech you, Zeus'
fair-haired child, Artemis,
queen of the beasts,
taking your pleasure now
in viewing a city of bold-hearted
men by the swirling Lethaeus[1]
(for you are not the shepherd
of a savage flock). . . . [11]

Drunk with desire again
I dive from Leucas' rock[2] to gray waves below. [12]

In an essay, *On the Characteristics of Animals,* Aelianus (2nd/3rd cent.
A.D.) says that those who maintain that does do not have antlers
disregard the authority of several poets, including Anacreon who

says of the female deer:

gently, as to a panic-stricken,
suckling fawn abandoned
in the woods by its antlered mother. [13]

Aelianus adds that

Aristophanes of Byzantium argues forcefully against those who change
the text, saying that "lovely" [*eroesses*] should be written instead of "ant-
lered" [*keroesses*].

Athenaeus preserves nine fragments of Anacreon's poetry. The first
comes in a discussion of the proper proportion of water to wine.

In Anacreon, we find one measure of wine to two of water:

Come and bring a bowl,
my boy, for me to drain
in a single breath, but add
ten ladles of water
to five of wine. I want
a nonviolent Bacchanal. [14]

Later he calls unmixed wine a Scythian drink:

I ask you again to stop
this Scythian drinking: taking
wine amid banging and howling.
Moderation is better and singing
beautiful songs to the gods. [15]

Athenaeus goes on to say that since thirst is the most insistent of
human desires, poets use it figuratively of various strong desires. The
examples he quotes include Archilochus' fragment 20 and this from
Anacreon:

You are kind to strangers, girl. I thirst. Let me drink. [16]

After quoting Xenophanes 4 to describe his own banquet, he adds
a similar passage by Anacreon:

No friend of mine stands by the wine bowl discoursing
    on battles and tearstained war.
I like a drinker whose mind is on pleasure, the Muses'
    splendid gifts, and Aphrodite's. [17]

Reverting to practical details, Athenaeus quotes Anacreon to prove
that in antiquity water was poured in the cup *before* wine.

Bring me water,
wine, and garlands,
boy! I want
to box with Eros! [18]

On the topic of luxury, Athenaeus mentions that Anacreon sati-
rized a parvenu named Artemon for his excesses:

In *Concerning Anacreon*, Chamaeleon of Pontus quotes the lines

Borne-about Artemon is
fair Eurypyle's passion, [19]

and explains that Artemon acquired the epithet "borne-about" from living
luxuriously and being carried around on a litter. In fact Anacreon de-
scribes how he rose from poverty to luxury in these lines:

Foul Artemon wore a knotted
headband, knucklebones for earrings
and leather over his ribs that once
was a poor shield's filthy cover.
He eked out a fraudulent living
with whores and bakers' wives,
was often bound to the stocks and wheel,
his back strapped bloody, hair
and beard plucked clean.
Now wearing golden earrings, he mounts
a carriage, with ivory parasol in hand,
just like the ladies. [20]

Later, the topic is love. Athenaeus says that many authorities em-
phasize the importance of one's lover's eyes. For example,

what is it that Anacreon says?

Boy with girlish eyes,
you hardly seem to notice
my efforts to catch you, oblivious
charioteer of my soul. [21]

In speaking of love poetry, Athenaeus touches on the chronology
of Sappho and Anacreon.

Hermesianax is wrong to think that Sappho and Anacreon lived at the same time. He was a contemporary of Cyrus and Polycrates; she, of Alyattes, Croesus' father. In *Concerning Sappho*, Chamaeleon mentions the popular belief that Anacreon addressed the following words to Sappho:

> Golden-haired Eros hits me
> again with a purple ball
> and dares me to play with the girl
> in elaborate sandals,
> but she hails from mighty Lesbos,
> thinks *my* hair, being gray,
> repulsive, and gapes at someone
> else, a woman. [22]

He goes on to say that Sappho spoke these words to Anacreon:

> Muse of the golden throne, you inspired
> the song the marvellous elder of noble
> Teos, land of fair women,
> delightfully sang.

But that this song is not by Sappho is clear to everyone. In fact, I think that Hermesianax was joking about their love affair. In his play *Sappho*, Diphilus the comedian made Archilochus and Hipponax her lovers.

Stobaeus preserves one fragment:

> Already my temples
> are gray, my head
> white. Young
> and charming no more.
> My teeth are antiques.
> Not much time
> is left. Often
> I sob, in fear of
> Tartarus; for Hades'
> pit is horrible,
> hard to descend
> and no coming back. [23]

Among the works of many later poets, the *Palatine Anthology* (10th cent. A.D.) contains a number of apparently false attributions to the early lyric poets, particularly Anacreon and Simonides. The following are two of the better epigrams assigned to Anacreon (see also Simonides' fragments 35 and 36).

All the city wept at the pyre of fierce
  Agathon, who died for Abdera.
Blood-loving Ares never killed his equal
  in the swirl of hateful battle. [24]

Of gallant friends, Aristocleides, I pity you the most.
You gave up your youth to save the fatherland from slavery. [25]

In an essay of unknown date, *Figures of Speech*, Herodian the rhetorician mentions the figure known as *polyptoton*. Possible only in inflected languages, it consists of repeating the same word several times with different grammatical endings. For example,

in Anacreon there is a threefold instance:

Yes I am Cleobulus' [*Kleobulou*] lover,
am mad for Cleobulus [*Kleobuloi*],
ogle Cleobulus [*Kleobulon*]. [26]

In Aristophanes' *Birds*, a poet arrives in the birds' kingdom, singing "Up to Olympus I fly on airy wings." A scholiast comments that

this is an adaptation of Anacreon's lines:

Up to Olympus I fly on airy wings:
Eros no longer wants to play with me. [27]

In Euripides' *Hecuba*, the captured Trojan women, who form the chorus, recall how on the night that Troy fell they took refuge at altars, scantily clad like Spartan girls. A scholiast remarks that

to go Dorian refers to women appearing naked, as in Anacreon:

Shedding your shift go Dorian. [28]

In the *Iliad* Poseidon, rebuked by Zeus, asserts that he and Hades share the governance of earth with him; Zeus is supreme only in heaven. This leads a scholiast to remark that

the people of Attica call the month of the winter solstice Poseideon. Ana-
creon:

> The month of Poseideon is here.
> Clouds are heavy with water;
> wild storms clatter. [29]

Near the end of the *Iliad,* we learn that the young Patroclus killed a
playmate in an argument over a game of dice. A scholiast informs us
that the term for dice, though normally masculine, is sometimes femi-
nine:

The feminine form is more Ionic:

> Eros' dice are fights and fits of madness.

Anacreon [i.e., the scholiast attributes this fragment to Anacreon]. [30]

In a victory ode, Pindar says that he sends songs to Olympian
victors the same way as a man might take a cup of wine and "pledge"
it to his son-in-law. A scholiast remarks,

Properly, pledge implies giving the cup as a present together with the
drink. Anacreon:

> Pledge me, friend,
> your slender thighs. [31]

Here *pledge* means *grant.*

In a different ode, Pindar refers to earlier days before "silver-
faced" songs were composed for profits. A scholiast adds that

Anacreon has said something similar. Pindar's reference may be to his
words. They are:

> Then Persuasion had no silver sheen. [32]

Simonides of Ceos

(6th/5th cent. B.C.)

Simonides was a native of Ceos, an island fifteen miles offshore from Attica. He probably first gained fame by composing songs for choruses of Cean boys, who competed at religious festivals. Eventually, he came to Athens and was, with Anacreon, one of the leading poets in the Pisistratid court. An epitaph that he wrote for Hippias' daughter attests to his good relationship with the tyrant's house (fragment 4). But even after the assassination of Hipparchus in 514 and the expulsion of Hippias in 510, Simonides remained in Athens, becoming an admirer of and even a spokesman for Athenian democracy. In fragment 22, he refers to the day that Hipparchus was assassinated as a bright one for the city. This may seem to cast a shadow on his character, since he had been Hipparchus' friend, but the apparently conflicting sentiments attributable to him are really not so different from those commonly held today: Pisistratus and his sons governed Athens well, but the democracy that replaced them was a great step forward. It is also possible that Hipparchus' character deteriorated over the years: his role in the events leading to his assassination does him no credit.[1]

Simonides stayed in Greece long enough to sing the praises of the heroes of the Persian war (fragments 1–3, 15, 20, 37). In old age, he retired to Sicily and the court of Hiero, tyrant of Syracuse, but none of his extant poetry seems to reflect his Sicilian experiences.

Simonides was a versatile and prolific poet; he composed victory odes, dirges, and elegies for the rich and famous in Athens and elsewhere. His poetry is engaged in the real world. He has a tendency to comment upon the opinions of others (fragments 6, 28, and 32). The philosophy of toleration expressed in his ode on virtue (fragments 5–13), the tenderness of "Danaë's Lullaby" (fragment 16), and many other passages mark him as one of the most thoughtful and sensitive of ancient Greek authors.

Quotations

The history written by Herodotus (5th cent. B.C.) tells the story of the Persian wars. Herodotus mentions Simonides in connection with the battle of Thermopylae (480 B.C.), which came about when King Leonidas of Sparta and an outnumbered allied force blocked the invading Persians at the pass of Thermopylae. Eventually, Leonidas dismissed the other allies, but he and his three hundred Spartans, the army of Thespiae, and a seer, Megistias of Acarnania, stayed and fought to the death. Afterwards, Herodotus says,

> They were all buried in the spot where they fell, both those who died before Leonidas dismissed part of the army and those who died afterwards. The inscriptions on their graves are as follows:
>
> > Here four thousand men of the Peloponnesus
> >   battled three million. [1]
>
> This is the epitaph for all the dead. Another is dedicated exclusively to the Spartans:
>
> > Tell them in Sparta, stranger, that here we lie,
> >   obedient to their commands. [2]
>
> That is for the Spartans. This is for the seer:
>
> > Here glorious Megistias lies, slain by the Medes
> >   when he crossed the Spercheius river.
> > A prophet, he clearly foresaw his death but refused
> >   to forsake his Spartan commander. [3]
>
> The Greek confederacy decorated their graves with inscriptions and pillars, except that Simonides, son of Leoprepes, made the inscription for the seer Megistias because of their friendship.

The attribution of all three epitaphs to Simonides began in antiquity and is widely accepted by modern scholars.

In his account of the fall of the Pisistratid tyranny in Athens, Thucydides (5th cent. B.C.) says that Hippias became more oppressive after the assassination of his brother Hipparchus and laid the groundwork for fleeing Athens. He went so far as to marry his daughter, Archedice, to the tyrant of Lampsacus, who was influential in the Persian court. Further,

[Archedice's] tomb still stands in Lampsacus, bearing this inscription:

> Here Archedice lies, child of Hippias, noblest
>   man of his generation in Greece.
> Daughter and wife, sister and mother of rulers,
>   her thoughts were ever humble. [4]

Attribution is based on the fact that Aristotle quotes line three as Simonides'.

In the *Protagoras*, Plato depicts a conversation between Socrates and Protagoras, who was the leading sophist of the day. The two debate the question of whether virtue can be taught, since Protagoras' fame rests, in effect, on his supposed ability to teach virtue. Protagoras prefers giving speeches to answering questions and only agrees to respond to Socrates' questions if Socrates will first answer his. When Socrates agrees, Protagoras stipulates that knowledge of poetry is highly important, and proceeds.

Somewhere Simonides addresses these words to the Thessalian Scopas, son of Creon:

> Becoming a truly good man
> solid in hands and feet and mind,
>   faultlessly fashioned, is difficult. [5]

Socrates says he knows the ode and considers it a beautiful composition, free of contradiction, but Protagoras challenges him.

Are you aware that as the ode continues, Simonides says:

> Nor does the saying of Pittacus ring
> true, though he was certainly wise;
> he said being virtuous was difficult. [6]

Protagoras says that this contradicts the beginning. First Simonides says that being virtuous is difficult; then he says it is not difficult but impossible. To explain away the apparent contradiction,

Socrates distinguishes between *becoming* good, i.e., going from a bad to a better state, which is difficult, and *being* absolutely and therefore permanently good, which is impossible. Only a philosopher would make such a distinction, and this was certainly not what Simonides had in mind. Plato probably intended the passage as a parody of excessively intellectual literary criticism. In any event, Socrates offers this paraphrase of Simonides:

> For a person who has become good to remain in this same state and to *be* a good man, as you say, O Pittacus, is impossible and not human:
>
> Only a god could have that privilege.
> A man overcome by a hopeless
> disaster always turns bad. [7]

After a digression, Socrates rephrases his summary of Simonides' idea:

> You say, O Pittacus, that it is difficult to *be* good. In fact, *becoming* good is difficult, but possible; being good is impossible, since:
>
> Whoever fares well is good,
> the unfortunate man is bad. [8]

According to Socrates, this is also what Simonides means by his later lines:

> best for the longest time
> are those whom the gods love. [9]

Socrates sees the whole poem as a reply to Pittacus. He says,

> All these things are relevant to Pittacus, as the next lines in the song show even more clearly.
>
> Therefore I shall not throw away
> my allotted time on an empty, impossible
> hope, looking for what cannot be,
> a man without fault among those of us
> who live on the spacious earth,
> but I will tell you if I find one. [10]

Throughout the whole poem he attacks Pittacus' saying with the same vehemence.

> I praise and love all men
> who do nothing disgraceful
> freely. Not even gods
> battle Necessity. [11]

Socrates interprets these lines in a peculiar fashion. Since it is obvious (to him) that no ever freely chooses to do evil, Simonides must mean that he *freely praises and loves* men who do nothing disgraceful. In other words, circumstances compel him to praise some tyrants who do disgraceful things; others he praises freely.

According to Socrates, Simonides' last point is that he is not criticizing Pittacus because he is judgmental. He says, in effect,

A man who is not evil is good enough for me, one:

> not going to lawless extremes, knowing
> that justice preserves the state,
> a man of sound mind. I will not
> find fault with him. The race
> of fools is infinite. [12]

Therefore, if someone took pleasure in criticizing, he could get his fill of criticizing them.

> All things are fair
> that are free from dishonor. [13]

This is not the equivalent of saying that all things are white which are free from black, which would be absurd in many ways. He means that he himself accepts normal behavior without criticizing it.

In his *Rhetoric*, Aristotle (4th cent. B.C.) makes the point that epithets may be used to elevate or demean a subject:

When the winner in a mule race offered Simonides a small fee, he refused it, as if he could not write poetry about mules. But when the man offered him a sufficient fee, he wrote:

> Hail, daughters of storm-footed steeds! [14]

In discussing Thermopylae, the historian Diodorus Siculus (1st cent. B.C.) says that the example of courage that Leonidas and his troops set in defeat was more valuable than any victory. Furthermore,

> not only historians but many poets have sung the praise of their courage. Simonides, the lyric poet, is one. He composed a worthy tribute, in which he says:

> Glorious the fortune, noble
> the fate of those who died at Thermopylae.
> Their tomb is an altar where mourning becomes a song of praise.
> Decay and all-conquering Time
> will never darken such a monument.
> This heroes' sepulcher won
> as its keeper the esteem
> of Hellas. The Spartan king, Leonidas,
> is proof: though he is gone, his courage
> ornaments his people and his fame flows on. [15]

Dionysius of Halicarnassus (1st cent. B.C.), the literary critic who preserves a famous Sapphic ode in his discussion of the selection of detail (Sappho fragment 8), also transmits an important fragment by Simonides. Dionysius is discussing the difference between poetry and prose. He says that good prose comes close to poetry by employing rhythms that suggest poetic meters without fully reproducing them. Conversely, poetry achieves the apparent freedom of prose by using clauses of different lengths, which begin in different parts of the metrical line. Simonides provides an example.

> Read the following passage phrase by phrase. The rhythm of the song will escape you and you will not be able to identify strophe, antistrophe, or epode. It will seem a piece of prose. Danaë[2] is being carried through the sea, lamenting her fate:

> Inside the ornate wooden chest,
> the gusting wind and heaving sea
> reduced her to panic and cheeks no longer dry.
> Taking Perseus in her circle of arms,
> she said, "My child,
> what trouble I have!
> But you sleep and dream,
> like the infant you are,
> suspended in this dark blue, starry night,

prisoner of joyless, bronze-studded wood.
The sea that towers overhead
on the passing wave
and the groaning wind
do not alarm you,
lying with your pretty face swaddled in purple.
But if this danger were danger to you,
you would lend your delicate ear to my words.
Sleep, child,
and let the sea and its infinite evil sleep.
Amendment could come,
father Zeus, from you.
If some word in this plea is bold
or lacking in justice,
forgive me." [16]

In a letter of consolation to a bereaved father, Plutarch argues that death is a blessing in disguise:

> If we enumerated all the anxieties of life, we would condemn it and affirm the opinion that prevails with some that dying is better than living. Simonides, for example:
>
>> Men's strength
>> is little, their griefs incurable, toil
>> follows toil throughout their short lives.
>> Death is looming over all, inescapable;
>> Good men draw its lot as often
>> as the evil do. [17]

Later in the same letter he adds the argument that length of life is less important than quality, since

> long and short seem no different when you consider eternity. As Simonides puts it,
>
>> a thousand or even ten thousand years is an infinitesimal point,
>> or rather the smallest portion of a point. [18]

In an essay on whether the elderly should participate in public affairs, Plutarch says that there are objections to beginning a political career late in life:

Simonides' saying,

> The city is the teacher of the man,

only applies to those who still have the time to be
re-educated and learn a new lesson. [19]

In an essay criticizing Herodotus' history, Plutarch takes issue
with the historian's statement that only the Spartans, Tegeans, and
Athenians actually fought in the battle of Plataea (479 B.C.), which
marked the final collapse of the Persian invasion. In fact, he says,
other cities played important roles:

> You can learn from Simonides the position of the Corinthians in fighting
> the barbarians at Plataea and how much credit they ultimately gained
> from the battle. He wrote:

>> Men from well-watered Ephyra[3] stood in the middle,
>>   masters of martial excellence,
>> and the rulers of Glaucus' town, the city of Corinth,
>>   who chose for their struggle the best
>> witness: the honored gold in the sky, which spreads
>>   abroad their fame and their fathers'. [20]

> He did not write these things for a chorus in Corinth or as part of a song
> for the city but recounted them in writing elegies about those events.

Aelius Aristides, a leading orator of the second century A.D., mentions
in a speech that he had incurred criticism for self-praise, but he says
that there are precedents for it. Simonides, the epitome of restraint,

> was bold enough to say:

>> No one, I say, can match Simonides in memory—

> No one else says this about Simonides, but it is a poem that he wrote
> about himself. And so that it will not seem that he is saying this when he
> is young and in his prime, he adds:

>> the octogenarian son of Leoprepes. [21]

Hephaestion's only citation of Simonides involves a rare license.
Hephaestion is making the point that metrical lines generally end
with complete words. Therefore, he says,

lines like these from Simonides' *Elegies* are objectionable:

> The day Hipparchus was slain by Harmodius and Aristo-
> geiton, Athens was bathed in light.[4] [22]

The lexicographer Pollux (2nd cent. A.D.) deals with words by seman-
tic category. In his entry on dogs, he lists some famous ones, remark-
ing that

> Simonides made Lycas, the Thessalian hunting dog, famous when he
> composed this epitaph for her grave:
>
> > Huntress, your bleached bones buried here
> >   still frighten the beasts! Great
> > Pelion, conspicuous Ossa and Cithaeron's high
> >   pastures know your excellence. [23]

In an epistle designed to convert the reader to Christianity, Theophi-
lus of Antioch (2nd cent. A.D.) lists Simonides as a pagan author who
believed in divine providence, citing the following lines as proof:

> No city, no man
> gains excellence without the gods;
> the master planner is a god, and nothing
> is free of grief. [24]

He also quotes Simonides as a pagan who believes that God's
punishment is swift:

> There is no evil
> that men should not expect; a god needs
> but a moment to scatter everything. [25]

In his discussion of luxury, Athenaeus quotes one Heracleides, the
hedonistic author of *On pleasure*, who wrote:

> The most intelligent men whose wisdom is held in the highest esteem
> believe that pleasure is the greatest good. For example, Simonides says:
>
> > With pleasure removed,
> > what life is appealing? What absolute power?
> > Not even the gods stir envy without it. [26]

Clement of Alexandria (2nd/3rd cent. A.D.) quotes verses by Simonides to show that trials and tribulations should not shake faith.

> The scripture says, "No one who trusts in Him will be put to shame."
> [Romans 10.11] Therefore Simonides writes well:
>
>> There is a story
>> that Virtue dwells atop a steep cliff,
>> in a precinct undefiled,
>> and never may be seen by eyes
>> of mortal until heartbreaking sweat
>> pours out of him
>> and he reaches the peak of manliness. [27]

Diogenes Laertius (3rd cent. A.D.) quotes Simonides in his brief life of Cleobulus, an obscure philosopher from Lindus on Rhodes:

> Some say [Cleobulus] composed the inscription on the tomb of Midas:
>
>> A maiden of bronze, I lie on Midas' tomb.
>> While water flows and trees grow tall,
>> the rising sun and bright moon shine,
>> rivers run and the ocean surges, I
>> shall remain on this, my tomb of great lamentation,
>> to tell passers-by that Midas is buried here.
>
> Their evidence is Simonides' song, where he says:
>
>> What man of intellect would praise Cleobulus, native of Lindus?
>> To rivers that flow forever, the flowers
>> of spring, the blaze of the sun and golden moon,
>> and the swirling sea he compared a monument's strength!
>> All things are weaker than gods, and human
>> hands break stone. That
>> was a fool's utterance. [28]

Stobaeus preserves six fragments.

> Time is the best touchstone; it uncovers the thought
>   that hides deep in the heart. [29]

> Time's teeth are sharp; they grind everything
>   down, no matter how hard. [30]

Not even the heroes of old, the semi-
divine sons of the gods, our masters,
reached old age without enduring
lives of toil, corruption, and danger. [31]

    Homer said one excellent thing:
"A generation of men is like a generation of leaves."
    But few who hear this with their ears
take it to heart; for the hope that grows in the breast
    of the child remains in every man.
So long as he keeps youth's beautiful bloom,
    he happily lays impossible plans.
He does not think he will ever age or die;
    in health, he has no fear of disease.
Those whose minds are so disposed are fools
    to forget that life and youth are brief.
But you, being so advised, should boldly indulge
    to the end of life in all its joys.[5] [32]

Being human, never declare what tomorrow will be
or say how long prosperity will last.
No dragonfly shifts as quickly. [33]

Everything, including great virtues and wealth,
    comes to one horrifying Charybdis. [34]

Dubious attributions to Simonides in the *Palatine Anthology* (10th cent.
A.D.) include the following.

Theodorus' Epitaph

By dying I gratify someone, who will gratify another.
    We are all indebted to death. [35]

I, Timocreon of Rhodes, an abusive, drunken
    glutton, rest in peace. [36]

In Aristophanes' *Peace*, the chorus sings, "If it is right, daughter of
Zeus, to honor the best and most renowned comic poet, our author
claims to be worthy of praise." A scholiast comments that these lines
are

an imitation of Simonides' words in his elegies:

> If, daughter of Zeus, it is right to honor the best,
> we Athenians did it alone. [37]

Bacchylides of Ceos

(6th/5th cent. B.C.)

Bacchylides was Simonides' nephew and a fellow native of Ceos. He was born late in the sixth century—exactly when is not known. It is tempting to think that he worked in close company with his uncle and accompanied him on his travels to Sicily. In any event, Bacchylides experimented with some of the same poetic genres that his uncle used, especially the victory ode, and soon rose to the top of his profession. His most famous poems are odes celebrating victories by the horses of Hiero, tyrant of Syracuse, in the Olympics of 476 and 468 repectively. Only a hundred lines of his poetry were known through various quotations until the discovery in 1896 of a papyrus containing the remnants of fourteen victory odes, including the ones just mentioned, and six dithyrambs—choral poems devoted exclusively to narrating mythical episodes. I have translated the odes of 476 and 468.

These two odes are typical of their genre, containing all the standard ingredients: brief mention of the victory being commemorated, a mythical narrative indirectly related to the victory, and maxims that more or less tie the whole together. Such poems seem very strange to modern readers. The genre was short-lived in antiquity, apparently invented by Simonides and dying with Pindar and Bacchylides, and there is nothing like it in modern literature. Complicating the matter is the proverbial obscurity of Pindar's language. To me the key to appreciating victory odes is the realization that the mythical episodes they incorporate are often quite humorous. These odes were meant to be sung at very festive occasions and were designed primarily as entertainment. Human nature has not changed so much that the poets who composed them would fail to exploit the rich humor of their mythical heritage to win some laughs. I return to this subject when introducing individual odes.

Little is known of Bacchylides' life: apparently, he and Pindar com-
peted for Hiero's favor. Since antiquity, critics have considered
Pindar the greater poet, but Bacchylides' simpler style may have
endeared him to Hiero more. Evidently, Hiero commissioned Bac-
chylides instead of Pindar to commemorate his greatest Olympic vic-
tory, that in the chariot race of 468. In his second Olympian Ode,
Pindar says, "A true poet knows many things by nature; learners
chatter in vain, furious in their verbosity, like a pair of crows cawing
at the godlike bird of Zeus." (86–88). Scholiasts to the passage claim
that the crows he had in mind were his rivals, Simonides and Bac-
chylides.

Besides honoring Hiero and a patron from southern Italy, Bac-
chylides wrote songs for Athenians, Ceans, and others from that
vicinity. Plutarch (*On Exile* 14.605C) says that the poet was exiled
from Ceos at one point and lived in the Peloponnesus. Nothing is
known about his death.

Victory Ode 3

Bacchylides' third victory ode commemorated a victory by Hiero's
team in a chariot race at Olympia in 468. Hiero was ailing at the time
and died the next year. Bacchylides tells the story of how, when
Sardis fell, the gods saved Croesus and his family from death by
self-immolation because of Croesus' piety. The implication is that
Hiero too can trust in the gods. But the incredible rescue is not meant
to be taken very seriously. Especially telling is the inclusion of the
unnecessary but comical detail that in response to Croesus' prayer,
Zeus hurries a cloud overhead and quenches the pyre with rain. Then
Apollo transports the whole family to land of the Hyperboreans.

Sing, O generous Clio, the praise   st.
of fertile Sicily's queen,
Demeter, her violet-wreathed girl,[1] and Hiero's
swift Olympian horses;

driven by Triumph and excellent Victory,   ant.
they flashed by the turbulent Alpheus   6
and placed the winner's garlands in the hands
of Deinomenes'[2] fortunate son.

The people shouted, "Thrice   ep.
happy man!   10
who obtained from Zeus
the Greeks' widest rule
and knows better than to cloak his towering
wealth in darkness."

Precincts teem with sacrificial processions,   st.
streets with hospitable feasts.   16
Gold glimmers amid rays
from graven tripods standing

in front of the temple, where Delphians care for   ant.
Phoebus' greatest shrine   20
by the Castalian fountain. Glorify God!
That is the crown of prosperity.

For the man who led horse-taming   ep.
Lydia's hosts,
when Zeus brought   25
the destined crisis to pass
and Sardis fell to the Persian army—
Croesus was saved by Apollo,

god of the golden sword. That unexpected   st.
day of grief, deciding   30
not to abide slavery, he built
a pyre facing the bronze

wall of his courtyard. With his virtuous wife   ant.
and daughters, who sobbed and tore
their elegant braids, he mounted, raised   35
his hands to the distant sky

and cried: "Overpowering deity,   ep.
where is the gods'
gratitude? Where
is Leto's lordly son?   40
Alyattes' palace has fallen. . . .
[Two lines are missing.]
The gold-bearing Pactolus is red
with blood, women are led away   45
from stately chambers to humiliation.

The hated is loved; death is sweetest."   ant.
He spoke and ordered his fastidious
servant to light the wood. The maidens
screamed and threw their hands   50

on their mother. Death foreseen   ep.
is bitterest for mortals,
but the fire no sooner
started to blaze than Zeus
positioned a cloud overhead and quenched   55
the golden flame.

Believe the will of the gods incapable   st.
of nothing! Apollo transported
the elderly man to the Hyperboreans and settled him
there with his slim-ankled daughters   60

in return for sending mankind's greatest   ant.
gifts to holy Pytho.
Not one of Hellas' lords, O most
praiseworthy Hiero, would dare

to claim he has sent more   ep.
gold to Loxias.   66
For one not fat
with envy it is easy to praise
a horse-loving martial man.
[Six lines are missing.]

... The lord Apollo   ant.
said to the son of Pheres[3]: "A mortal,   77
you must be firm in two

convictions: that tomorrow's sun   ep.
is the last you will see   80
and that you will live
in luxury for fifty years."
Take pleasure in holy works,
the highest profit.

To the wise my words have meaning: the sky   st.
is undefiled; the sea's water   86
does not decay and gold is joy,
but a man may not cast off

gray age and recover the bloom   ant.
of youth. Virtue's sheen   90
never fades away like the body's;
the Muse preserves it, Hiero,

and yours are the finest flowers   ep.
of wealth. Silence
is not success'
ornament. By truth will live   95
the tale of your glories and the gift of the sweet-tongued
nightingale of Ceos.

Victory Ode 5

The fifth ode commemorates an earlier victory by Hiero's entry in a horse race in the Olympic games of 476. This must be one of the most famous horse races in literature, since it is also the subject of Pindar's first Olympian Ode (translated below). The steed, Phereni-cus (Victory-bearer), is lavishly praised by both poets.

In the mythical section of his poem, Bacchylides creates one of the most ironic moments in Greek literature. Heracles is introduced in the land of the dead, where he has gone to fetch Hades' three-headed dog, Cerberus. En route, he meets the statuesque ghost of Meleager, the hero of the Calydonian boar hunt, who has been killed by his mother's action because of a feud with her brothers. Heracles elicits Meleager's long sad, tale and is, we are told, moved to tears by it, but his reply is none too sensitive. Besides being a hard-working hero, Heracles is a legendary womanizer. He tells Meleager in effect that life is hard and asks him whether he happens to have any maiden sisters. He wouldn't mind marrying a girl with Meleager's looks! As Bacchylides' audience knew, Meleager's sister was Deianira, who was destined to marry Heracles and unwittingly to cause his death when he became involved with yet another woman.[4] But Bacchylides ends his narrative abruptly when Meleager answers Heracles.

Commander by good fortune	st.
of the horse-twirled Syracusans,	
you will correctly interpret	
this sweet dedication of the violet-crowned Muses,	
if anyone on earth	5
could do so. Resting your judicious	
mind from its cares, direct	
your thoughts this way.	
By aid of the buxom Graces, your friend	
and famous servant	10
of Urania[5] with her golden crown	
has woven a song;	
from sacred isle he sends it	
to your famous city.	
He wishes to pour	15
from his heart praise of Hiero.	ant.
Slicing the sky overhead,	

brown wings beating,
an eagle, the messenger of sovereign Zeus,
god of thunder,   20
brims with courage, trusting
his strength, but shrill songbirds
tremble with fear.
Mountain peaks do not deter him
or crashing waves   25
on the tireless sea. He draws
all eyes, traveling
endless space, as a zephyr's
breath smooths
his delicate plumage.   30

And countless paths are open to me   ep.
in every direction
to hymn your virtue, thanks to dark-haired
Victory and bronze-plated Ares,
O noble sons of Deinomenes.[6]   35
May God not weary of doing you kindness!
Dawn the golden knows
how tawny Pherenicus, who runs
like a sudden storm,
prevailed by the banks of the turbulent Alpheus   40

and holy Pytho. As Earth   st.
is my witness, I swear that never
has dust raised in the struggle
by horses in front dirtied his face
on the final sprint.   45
He throws himself forward,
a rival to Boreas gusting,
but heeding his driver,
and wins anew for kindly Hiero.
He is blessed who has   50
a share of god-given glory
and adds to his enviable
fate a prosperous life.
No mortal is fortunate
in every way.   55

Once, they say, the unconquered   ant.
breaker of gates, seedling
of Zeus of the glittering bolt,
Heracles entered Persephone's palace
to bring the saw-toothed   60
hound, child of terrible

Echidna, from Hades to daylight.
On the banks of Cocytus,
he met the souls of unfortunate mortals,
swirling like leaves   65
in the wind on pastures and glistening
headlands of Ida.
One shape stood out among them,
the steadfast Meleager,
Porthaon's descendant.   70

Seeing the glint of his armor, Alcmena's   ep.
wondrous hero
stretched his shrill bowstring to hook,
undid the quiver's flap,
and selected a bronze-tipped   75
arrow, but knowing him well Meleager's
spirit came forward
to face him and said, "Great
Zeus' son,
stand still and gentle your temper.   80

Why waste the strength of your hands   st.
shooting a brutal shaft
at the souls of men who have died?
You have nothing to fear." Amphitryon's son
said in amazement,   85
"Who was the god or mortal
who raised a seedling such
as you? And where?
And who was your killer? Beautifully girded
Hera might send him   90
at me, but that concerns
fair Pallas."
In tears Meleager replied:
"It is hard for men
to make the gods   95

alter decisions; or else   ant.
my father, Oeneus, driver
of horses, had stemmed the anger
of holy Artemis[7] wreathed by flowers,
when he made supplication   100
by slaughter of numerous goats
and cattle with russet backs;
but the maiden's anger
was not overcome. She unleashed a mighty,
savage boar   105

on Calydon's fair land.
Overflowing with strength,
he tusked the vineyards to pieces,
slaughtering sheep
and any man in his way.   110

We princes of Greece relentlessly warred   ep.
against him for six
consecutive days. When a deity granted
Aetolia success, we buried
the men the monstrously snorting   115
pig had killed on his violent forays,
including Ancaeus and Agelaus,
the best of my virtuous brothers,
of those whom Althaea
bore to Oeneus in his storied halls.   120

And deadly fate destroyed   st.
still more. Not yet had Leto's
daughter, the hostile huntress,
ended her anger: we fought the stubborn
Curetes fiercely   125
for the sake of the splendid hide.
Those I killed included
with many others
Iphiclus and noble Aphares, my swift
maternal uncles.   130
Bold Ares sees
no friends in battle.
Spears are blind and bring
death to the enemy
chosen by fate.   135

But the wrathful child of Thestius,   ant.
my mother by evil fate,
refused to consider this truth;
stranger to fear, she plotted my death.
From a graven chest   140
she retrieved the log of swift
destruction and set it on fire.[8]
By fate's design,
it marked the end of my life. I chanced
to be stripping the faultless   145
body of Clymenus, Daipylus'
valiant son,
which I found in front of the towers

of Pleuron; I ran
for the massive, ancient   150

city. I knew I was losing strength,   ep.
my soul was shrinking.
Aiai! Breathing my last, I wept
for the loss of my splendid youth."
They say that only then   155
Amphitryon's son, fearless in battle,
moistened his eye, from pity
for the fate of the sorrowful man.
He answered him thus:
"Not to be born is best for mortals,   160

and never seeing the sun's   st.
light. But since there is nothing
to gain by lamenting such deeds,
it is better to speak of plans for the future.
So tell me, does warlike   165
Oeneus have in his halls
a virgin daughter like
to you in stature?
I would happily make her my wife."
The soul of Meleager,   170
steadfast in battle, replied,
"At home, I left
Deianira, a dewy-necked girl,
innocent of golden
Aphrodite's charms."   175

White-armed Muse, Calliope,   ant.
stop your sturdy chariot
here! Praise Zeus,
Cronus' son, the gods' commander,
and the unwearied stream   180
of Alpheus, mighty Pelops,
and Pisa where the feet of famous
Pherenicus prevailed
in running and he brought to towering Syracuse
foliage of joy   185
for Hiero. Praise true
grace and push
envy away with both
hands when any
mortal prospers.   190

A man of Boeotia, the Muses' servant,   ep.
Hesiod said

that he whom the deathless gods honor
is attended by fame among mortals.
I am persuaded with ease   195
to send these words of praise straight
to Hiero, the ground in which
the roots of blessings flourish.
Zeus, father
supreme, guard them in peace and quiet.   200

Pindar of Thebes

(6th/5th cent. B.C.)

Pindar was born about 520 in Cynoscephalae, a village on the outskirts of Thebes. Like Simonides and Bacchylides, he wrote choral songs for various patrons. His earliest datable poem was written for a Thessalian noble in 498 B.C. He must have achieved the status of a major poet by 476, when he like Bacchylides wrote an ode honoring the Olympic victory by Hiero's horse. His latest poems are dated to 446, and he is thought to have died in 438.

Pindar's works were published in seventeen volumes in antiquity. They included hymns, dithyrambs, processional songs, *partheneia*, songs for dancing, encomiums, dirges, and victory odes. Only the victory odes have been preserved by a regular manuscript tradition. I have translated two of his best known victory odes.

Greek athletic competitions were connected with religious festivals. Pindar's odes are arranged and titled by the festival at which the victories that they commemorate were won. Thus, his fourteen Olympian Odes refer to the famous festival of Zeus at Olympia; his twelve Pythian Odes to the festival of Apollo at Delphi; and his eight Isthmian Odes to a festival of Poseidon in Corinth. The eleven "Nemean Odes" include eight referring to a festival of Zeus in Nemea (in Argos), and three on miscellaneous occasions. My selections are Olympian 1 and Pythian 9.

Pindar is generally agreed to be a great poet; he is certainly a challenging one. His poetry is full of mixed metaphors, cryptic maxims, and other obscurities. Read with patience, however, he is usually found to be saying something interesting. As in the case of Bacchylides, I think that there is a rich and undervalued vein of humor in his mythical narrations.

The First Olympian Ode

It is difficult to understand how the mood of high seriousness that
many scholars bring to the study of Pindar could survive acquain-
tance with this, his most famous poem, which celebrates Hiero's
victory in 476. After he praises the horse Pherenicus, a reference to
Pisa, the district in which Olympia was located, gives Pindar his
excuse to recount a myth concerning the hero Pelops, a Lydian by
birth, who migrated to Pisa and according to some founded the
Olympic Games. Pindar says that he is going to introduce some
changes into the story to avoid insulting the gods. According to the
tale known to the poet's audience, Pelops' father was Tantalus, a
favorite son of Zeus. Invited to a banquet of the gods, Tantalus de-
cided to show them up by tricking them into eating human flesh and
he butchered Pelops for this purpose. Not fooled, the gods con-
demned Tantalus to eternal misery in Hades and reassembled Pelops.
Since his shoulder was missing, they made him an ivory replace-
ment. Poseidon fell in love with the reconstructed Pelops and gave
him a flying chariot. Just at this juncture, many young heroes wanted
to marry Hippodamia, the daughter of King Oenomaus of Pisa. To
win her hand, a suitor had to defeat her father in a chariot race with
death being the penalty for failure. Details vary, but Pelops used
Poseidon's gift to win the race, Hippodamia, and the kingdom of
Pisa.

Pindar says that he is going to revise the tale, since stories about
the gods should be decorous. In the alternate version which he pro-
poses, Tantalus invited the gods to a "perfectly proper" feast at his
house. There Poseidon fell in love with the young Pelops and ab-
ducted him. When Pelops was missed, an envious neighbor invented
the story of his being cut up and eaten. Pindar summarizes the envi-
ous neighbor's supposedly objectionable story with gusto, specifying
that Pelops' flesh was served as a dessert, and throughout the poem
he keeps reminding us of it by using culinary metaphors: Tantalus
could not *digest* his good fortune; young Pelops did not want to *stew*
in obscurity. So Pelops was not really eaten, just ravished. Then
when he grew up, he obtained Poseidon's help in defeating Oeno-
maus in return for his sexual favors.

Obviously, there is no sense in which Pindar's revised version
actually puts Poseidon or Pelops in a more dignified light. (The

Greeks did not view pederasty as intrinsically perverse, but sexually impulsive actions had the same comic value for them as for us.) Pindar's purpose is entertainment, not pious edification.[1]

The First Olympian Ode

Water is best and gold, conspicuous as fire	st.
blazing at night, is swaggering wealth's preeminent form,	
but if you wish	
to sing of games,	
my heart, look for	5
no luminous star in the empty sky by day outwarming the sun,	
or a contest to speak of nobler than the Olympian.	
There the minds of poets are filled with songs	
of praise for noisily extolling	
Zeus when they come to the wealthy	10
and blessed hearth of Hiero,	

who wields a righteous scepter in the fruitful land   ant.
of Sicily, plucking the peaks of achievement in every endeavor
and taking delight
in the finest of music,   15
such as it is
our custom to play at his gracious table. Now lift from its hook the Dorian[2]
lyre, if Pisa's splendor and that of Pherenicus
subjected your mind to thoughts of the sweetest sort,
when he galloped beside the Alpheus,   20
pressing forth ungoaded,
and linked to Victory his lord,

the horse-loving Syracusan king. His fame shines bright   ep.
in the well-manned colony founded by Lydian Pelops,
with whom the mighty earthshaking Poseidon   25
fell in love, when Clotho[3] plucked him from the cleansing cauldron,
complete with glistening ivory shoulder.
Wonders are many, and yet at times
utterance beyond the true   28b
account, tales adorned with artful lies mislead.

The very Grace who gentles everything for mortals   st.
in conferring her honor often contrived to make   31
the incredible seem true;
but the future will give
the wisest testimony.
When it comes to the gods, seemly tales are apt, and resentment
                                                                            is less.   35

So I shall make the novel assertion, Pelops,
that when your father invited the gods to a perfectly
proper feast in Sipylus
to pay their hospitality back,
the lord of the trident, smitten   40

by love, snatched you away on his golden chariot   ant.
up to the exalted home of widely honored Zeus,
whom Ganymede later
visited on
a similar mission.   45
After you disappeared and far-flung searches failed to restore
                                         you to mother,
one of your envious neighbors was quick to whisper
the tale that the gods had cut you to pieces, put
your flesh in boiling water,
then passed the bowl from table   50
to table, and ate you for dessert.

Far be it from me to accuse the blessed gods of gluttony!   ep.
Lack of profit has often befallen the slanderous.
And if ever Olympus' guardians honored
a mortal, that man was Tantalus, but he could not digest   55
his rich good fortune. By greed
he incurred ruination, the boulder his father
suspended above his head.[4]   57b
Eternally yearning to cast it away he misses all pleasure.

He has this hopeless life of never-ending toil,   st.
one among four[5], because he gave his drinking companions   60
ambrosia and nectar,
which he stole from the gods,
who had used them to make him
immortal. A man who expects his deeds to escape divinity
                                         miscalculates.
Therefore the gods dismissed his son, sending him   65
back among the short-lived race of men.
As he neared the prime of youth,
and whiskers darkened his chin,
he saw a chance to marry

and schemed to take from her father, lord of Pisa,   ant.
glorious Hippodamia. Going alone to the sea one night,   71
he called on the thundering
lord of the trident,
who appeared at his elbow.
He said, "Come now, Poseidon, if Cypris' favors earn a bit   75

of grace, ground the brazen spear of Oenomaus,
send me to Elis aboard your speediest car,
and put me in reach of Victory.
The man delays his daughter's
wedding; thirteen suitors   80

have died. Great danger does not attract a coward.   ep.
Since death must come, why sit in the dark, stewing
in nameless old age, accomplishing nothing,
lacking all honors? This is the contest for me
to enter. Grant me dear success."   85
Such was his speech, and it had its effect
on the god; glorifying him,   86b
Poseidon presented a chariot of gold and tireless horses with wings.

He mastered the might of Oenomaus and a maidenly bride.   st.
She bore him six leaders of men bursting with virtues.
Lying by Alpheus,   90
he partakes of the shining
blood of the victims
in a well-attended tomb beside the teeming altar. And the glory casts
its light afar that is won in Pelops' Olympian
races, where speed of feet and strength at its height,   95
shirking no effort, compete.
For the rest of his life the winner
enjoys a sweet serenity

in competition's realm, though each day's present blessing   ant.
is the highest good that anyone attains. Now I must crown him   100
with a song of horses,
an Aeolian melody.[6]
I trust I shall never
wrap in the glorious folds of my song a patron who so understands
what nobility is or has superior power.   105
Some god is guarding your interests; you are the object,
Hiero, of all his concern.
Unless he departs prematurely,
I think I will sing a sweeter

victory song for a chariot[7], assuming I find a smooth   ep.
path of words by the sunny hill of Cronus;   111
my Muse is nursing a most valorous shaft.
Various kinds of greatness exist, but the summit belongs
to kings. Cast your gaze no farther!
May you remain exalted all
your days and I, a friend   115b
to victors and celebrated poet among Greeks of every land.

The Ninth Pythian Ode

The Ninth Pythian Ode commemorates a victory by Telesicrates, son of Carneiades, in a strenuous event: a race in full armor. Teleiscrates was a citizen of a Cyrene, a wealthy Greek colony on the northern coast of Africa, in modern Libya. Pindar tells the myth of the foundation of the city in a way that illustrates the fluidity of mythical thought. Cyrene was originally a tomboyish maiden in Thessaly. Apollo brought her to Africa, married her, and made her the ruler of a city named after her. By this marriage, the maiden seems to become a goddess whose identity is merged with that of her namesake city.

The ode is full of light-hearted romance. The urgency of love is a recurring motif. Apollo immediately desires Cyrene when he sees her wrestling with a lion. Chiron, the wise centaur, persuades him to go through with the formality of a marriage, but that only takes Apollo a single day.

Seemingly as an afterthought, Pindar tells the story of how a Cyrenean hero named Alexidamus won his bride in a footrace. The bride's father supposedly modeled the contest after Danaus, who disposed of forty-eight unmarried daughters on a single morning in a similar way.

I wish to announce a Pythian victory   st.
bearing a brazen shield
and proclaim with the help of the buxom Muses
the name of Telesicrates, man of wealth and ornament
of horse-driving Cyrene, whom Leto's long-haired son snatched as a
                                                  wild-hearted virgin   5
from Pelion's windy recesses, carried aboard
his golden chariot, and made
the queen of a land most fertile and rich in sheep,
to flourish and settle a third well-favored continent.[8]

Aphrodite rose to her silvery feet   10 ant.
to welcome her Delian friend,
guided the chariot lightly, and shed
a becoming modesty upon their union's sweetness,
joining in marriage's common bond a god and the daughter of mighty
                                                              Hypseus,
who was at the time the king of the rowdy Lapiths,   15
a hero and grandson of Ocean,
born in the fabled valleys of Pindus to a nymph,

Creousa, daughter of Earth, who found her joy

in the bed of Peneus. Hypseus brought up   ep.
a child, the fair-armed Cyrene, who hated pacing back and forth by
                          the loom   20
and the feasts that amused the other females at home.
She preferred doing battle with brazen
spears and a sword, wreaking destruction on savage
beasts (and thus providing great
peace of mind for her father's cattle). She wasted little   25
time on the sweetness
of sleep, which touched her eyelids at dawn.

Far-darting Apollo, lord of the quiver,   st.
happened upon her alone,
wrestling a monstrous lion, unarmed.   30
With a shout he summoned Chiron[9] at once from his halls.
"Come out of your sacred cave, son of Philyra, and see power and
                          might
displayed by woman. What strife! What a dauntless expression!
A girl whose heart is higher
than hardship, whose thoughts do not flutter in the winds of fear!   35
Who gave her birth? Which family tree produced

this twig among these shadowy dells?   ant.
She smacks of boundless courage.
Would it be holy to lay upon her
my glorious hand and reap her luscious grass   40
unmarried?"[10] A laugh relaxed the inspired centaur's brow. With no
                          hesitation
he said: "It takes some time to find the keys
of persuasion unlocking a holy
love, and shame prevents both gods and men
from openly rushing upon the pleasures of bed.   45

In short, your good-natured passion has made you,   ep.
whom falsehood may not touch, inclined to make a mistake, and you
                          ask of the girl's
ancestry, lord, though you know everyone's fate
and every path and how many
leaves the earth produces in spring, and how many   50
grains of sand tumble in rivers
and sea or blow in the wind, and what the future will bring,
and from where it will bring it.
But I shall speak, since I must, in Wisdom's

face. You came to this grove as a bridegroom;   55 st.
over the sea you are destined

to bear her to Zeus' loveliest garden.
There you will make her a queen, gathering island
folk on a hill in the midst of a plain.[11] Libya, queen of broad meadows,
will graciously receive your illustrious bride in a palace   60
of gold and bequeath as lawfully
hers a portion of land neither unburdened
by fruits of every kind nor a stranger to beasts.

She will bear you a son, whom glorious Hermes   ant.
will take from his mother and give   65
to the Hours, high on their thrones, and Earth.
Beholding the newborn babe lying on their knees,
they will moisten his little lips with drops of ambrosia and nectar to make
                                        him a god,
a Zeus, a holy Apollo, joy to men,
to flocks their closest companion,   70
'The Hunter' to some, 'The Herdsman' or 'Aristaeus'[12] to others."
So speaking he armed him for marriage's joyous completion.

When gods decide to make haste,   ep.
action is swift, and journeys brief. It was settled that day. The two were
                                        united
in Libya's golden chamber, on the site of her loveliest   75
city, glorious in competition.
And now in holy Pytho, Carneiades' son
has married Cyrene to thriving Success.
His victory made her shine, and she will kindly welcome
to the land of beautiful   80
women an importer of Delphian glory.

Where virtue is great, legends are many,   st.
and the lengthy embellishment of minor
adventures amuses the wise,[13] but doing
what the occasion demands is best, which Thebans[14]   85
saw Iolaus do that time he regained his youth and ravaged Eurystheus'
                                        head
with the edge of his sword, and they hid him beneath the earth
by the tomb of his father's father,
Amphitryon, the sown men's foreign friend,
who settled in Thebes full of white horses.   90

Embraced by him and by Zeus, the prudent   ant.
Alcmena, laboring once,
delivered twins, mighty in battle.
Only a mute would fail to mention Heracles
or omit a description of Dirce's water that nourished him and
                                        Iphicles too.   95

But I shall lead their revel, since they fulfilled
my prayer. Abide with me,
pure light of the boisterous Graces. Thrice
on Aegina and Nisus' hill, he glorified this city,[15]

by achievement escaping reticent frustration.   100 ep.
So let no townsman, friend or foe, conceal a deed well done in the public
sphere and break the command of the sea's old man[16]
to give a just amount
of hearty praise to a rival's noble achievements.
I have often seen you victorious in Pallas'   105
seasonal rites and noted how all the Athenian virgins
silently prayed
for you as a husband or son, Telesicrates;

so too at Olympic games, and those   st.
of the full-breasted Earth and local   110
contests. But while I am drinking my fill
of songs, somebody says that I owe it to him
to revive his ancestors' glory, those men who went to Antaeus' city, Irasa,
for the sake of a Libyan wife; for they came to court
a fair-tressed, illustrious maiden.   115
Among the champions seeking her hand were numerous
kinsmen and numerous strangers. Such awe her beauty

inspired. They merely wanted to harvest   ant.
the fruit of the youth she wore
like a golden crown, but her father engendered   120
a wedding for greater glory. He heard that in Argos
Danaus[17] devised the quickest method to marry his forty-eight
                                        maiden daughters.
It was over by noon. He deployed the entire chorus
at the finish line of a track
and told his prospective sons-in-law all to decide   125
with their feet which of the girls each one would get.

And that was the way the Libyan fit   ep.
his child with a husband. He put her behind a line, decked out as the final
                                        goal,
and announced in their midst that whoever ran to her first,
touching her dress, could take her.   130
Alexidamus' nimble sprint left the others behind.
Holding the modest maiden's hand,
he led her through the milling Numidian horsemen, who tossed
garlands and leaves,
but he was used to victory wreaths.   135

Corinna of Tanagra

(5th cent. B.C. [?])

The most renowned poetess of ancient Greece, after Sappho, was Corinna, who came from a town in Boeotia named Tanagra. Her life is the subject of a complex and unresolved debate among experts. Ancient sources say that she was a contemporary of Pindar and that she defeated him at least once in a music contest. In his description of Tanagra, the geographer Pausanias (2nd cent. A.D.) writes.

> A monument to Corinna, Tanagra's only composer of songs, occupies a conspicuous position in the city and there is a painting of her in the city's gymnasium. She is binding her head with a ribbon because of a victory that she won over Pindar. I think that she won the victory on account of her dialect, because she did not sing in Doric like Pindar but in language that the Aeolians would understand, and also because she was the most beautiful woman of her age, if one can judge by the painting (9.22.3).

Alone among major authors, Corinna wrote in the Boeotian dialect, a subdivision of Aeolic.

Doubt was cast on the historicity of Pausanias' story by the renowned scholar Edgar Lobel, who pointed out that Corinna's spelling conformed to Boeotian as it was written approximately 300 B.C., not in Pindar's lifetime.[1] Lobel believed that Corinna was a Hellenistic poet who affected an archaic style and that the story of her victory over Pindar is sheer anachronistic fantasy. Stressing the fact that the story of her rivalry with Pindar seems to have been well established in antiquity, other scholars have argued that while she lived in the fifth century, her poems' orthography was "modernized" in a third- or second-century edition of her work. Opinion on the issue seems evenly divided at the present time.

Only two meaningful fragments from Corinna's poetry survive. Both are preserved on a second-century A.D. papyrus and deal with

Boeotian myths in a light-hearted manner. In the first, two moun-
tains, Helicon and Cithaeron, have a singing contest. As the fragment
becomes comprehensible, one of them is concluding his song about
the infancy of Zeus, who had to be hidden from his father Cronus.
Afterwards, at the Muses' direction, the gods vote on a winner by
secret ballot. Cithaeron wins. Helicon is so upset that he smashes a
huge boulder to bits.

In the second fragment, a Boeotian river god, Asopus, is looking
for his nine missing daughters. A seer named Acraephen tells him
that they were all abducted by gods: three by Zeus, three by Apollo,
two by Poseidon, and one by Hermes. But he should not be upset:
his daughters' sons will be famous heroes.

Judging by these fragments, Corinna's style was simple, like Bac-
chylides', and for that reason she may indeed have had greater ap-
peal than Pindar to some judges.

Papyrus Fragments

. . . "But Curetes[2]
hid the goddess' holy
babe in a cave where Cronus
could not find him, that time
he was stolen by blessed Rhea,
which magnified her honor among
immortals." Such was his song.
The Muses instructed the gods
to cast their votes in secret,
in urns of glistening gold.
They all jumped up together.
Cithaeron had the edge;
Hermes breaking the news
told him the crown he longed
to have was his, and the gods
encircled his brow with garlands.
His thoughts were filled with cheer,
but Helicon was overwhelmed by the bitter
pangs of defeat. He wrenched
a sheer cliff loose
from the mountain, which shuddered pathetically,
then raising the boulder he shattered it
into a million pebbles. [1]

"Father Zeus, our king,
has taken three of your daughters,
and three are married to the lord
of the sea, Poseidon. Apollo
governs the beds of two,
and one belongs to Hermes,
Maia's son. At the urging
of Eros and Cypris those gods
crept in your house and abducted
all nine of the maidens.
In the course of time they will bear
a race of heroic demigods
and shall dwell in far-flung places.
From the oracular art of the ageless tripod . . .
. . . this privilege . . .
I, the prophet Acraephen,
the best of my fifty valiant
brothers, received as my lot
the holy sanctuary's truth.
Euonymus was the first
Apollo endowed with the gift
of speaking his tripods' oracles.
Poseidon's son, Hyrieus
gained the honor next
by driving Euonymus out,
but Orion, who sired me,
reacquired the land that was his,
and now he frequents the sky.
. . . this honor . . .
. . . I utter
the certitudes of oracular speech.
Your part is to yield to the gods,
freeing your mind. . . .
Your sons-in-law are divine."
So spoke the reverend seer.
With a sigh of relief Asopus
clutched the prophet's hand,
and tears ran from his eyes
as he spoke these words in reply. . . . [2]

The Theognidean Anthology
(7th – 5th century B.C.)

The last poems in this volume are a selection from elegiac epigrams attributed to Theognis. The whole collection totals 1389 lines divided variously by modern editors into three hundred to four hundred separate poems, ranging in length from single couplets to thirty-line compositions.

Theognis was a noble from Megara. His values and concerns were similar to Alcaeus'; he too felt that his position and property were threatened by political developments. He addressed his poems to a protégé, whom he calls Cyrnus or Polypaide (son of Polypas), giving advice and complaining about the character of the people who are gaining power. Ancient encyclopedias said that he lived in the middle of the sixth century. The conditions that he described could have existed in Megara at that time but they fit the end of the seventh century better, when the city was taken over by a tyrant named Theagenes, a champion of the poor. Hence, M. L. West dates him to around 620–600 B.C.

The collection of Theognis' verse that has come down to us was expanded in antiquity into an anthology of elegiac poetry. In its current state, it includes poems attributed on good authority elsewhere to Tyrtaeus, Mimnermus, Solon, and Phocylides. Conflicting chronological indications, including likely references to the Persian Wars, and the contrasting treatment of similar themes also favor the assumption that different authors and generations are represented. The last 150 lines, set apart as "Book II" in the manuscripts, consist mostly of tepidly erotic poems addressed by a man, who may or may not have been Theognis, to an unnamed boy, possibly but not necessarily Cyrnus.

In general the Theognidean poems are prosaic. There are a few arresting images and marvelously terse epigrams, but the collection's greatest value lies in its detailed portrait, warts and all, of the Archaic Greek aristocrat.

I have provided titles for the epigrams for ease of comprehension. There are no titles in the actual manuscripts, nor any indication where one poem ends and another begins.

19–26 Theognis' "Seal"

For the sake of my art, let a seal[1] be placed on these verses,
    Cyrnus, so no one can steal them
or replace the noble original with inferior copy.
    All will say, "These
are the words of Theognis of Megara, famous everywhere."
    But not all the townsmen are pleased.
No wonder, Polypaide. Not even Zeus can please
    everyone with rain or shine.

39–52 The Imminence of Tyranny

Cyrnus, the city is pregnant. I fear the birth
    of one who will chastise our arrogance.
The people are virtuous still, but their leaders are slipping
    into the depths of vice.
The good have never destroyed a city, Cyrnus,
    but the wicked, turning to force,
ruin the state with judgments that favor injustice
    for personal profit and power.
Do not expect that our city, however peaceful,
    will stay quiet for long
when wicked men acquire a taste for profit
    produced by public evil.
Then factions come, violence, and tyrants—things
    I hope this city dreads.

53–68 The Nouveaux Riches

This city is still the same, but the people have changed.
    Those ignorant of trials and laws
before, who wore out the hides of goats on their ribs,
    living like deer in the wilderness,
are gentlemen now, Polypaide, and former nobles
    are beggars, an unendurable sight. . . .[2]
They cheat and mock each other without understanding
    the principles of good and evil.
Polypaide, do not for any amount befriend
    one of them in earnest.

In conversation, seem to be a friend to them all,
    but trust them in no serious
matter. If you do, you will learn that lowborn hearts
    are disloyal when put to the test.
They turn to deception and tangled lies as quickly
    as men in desperate danger.

83–86 Integrity Is Rare

If you gathered all the men in whose speech and eyes
    genuine honor resided,
whom profit could not lead to shameful action,
    a single ship would hold them.

149–50 Virtue Better than Wealth

Fate can enrich the utterly worthless, Cyrnus;
    excellence is reserved for the few.

151–52 Pride before a Fall

The gods send Arrogance to attend an evil
    man marked for destruction.

173–78 Poverty

Nothing defeats a good man like poverty,
    not gray age or fever.
Avoid it though you must jump from a high cliff,
    Cyrnus, or into the sea.
An impoverished man can neither act nor speak.
    His tongue has been put in chains.

183–92 Money versus Breeding

We look for well-bred rams, donkeys, and horses
    and want to mate them well;
but a nobleman gladly weds the lowborn daughter
    of a lowborn man for money;
and a woman willingly marries a scoundrel with riches,
    preferring "prosperous" to "good."
Property means honor; the classes intermarry;
    riches jumble lineage.
The city's degeneration should not surprise you, Polypaide,
    when nobility is bred with wickedness.

213–18 Be a Chameleon

Cyrnus,[3] adjust your character for every friend;
    blend your temperament with his.
Be like the artful octopus, whose appearance mimics
    the rock by which he lies.
Shift here and there; change your complexion.
    Better wise than inflexible.

237–54 Poetry Confers Immortality

I have given you wings with which to fly
    over the earth and sea,
effortlessly, and be wherever feasting is,
    your name on every tongue.
Young men whom others love shall sing
    rousing songs in your honor
to the tune of their pipes. And when you go
    to Hades' mournful palace,
not even in death will you lose your glory. Your name
    cannot perish, Cyrnus;
Men will remember it always, and you will travel
    Hellas, the islands, across
the barren sea, needing no horses. The gifts
    of the violet-crowned Muses will bear you.
While earth and sun endure, you will be sung of
    by all who care for song.
And yet you do not respect me, but tell me lies
    as if I were an infant.

271–78 Ungrateful Children

Ruinous age, youth, and the other gifts
    of the gods are fair, but a most
excessive evil, worse than death and every
    illness combined, occurs
when you raise your children, providing all their needs,
    and sacrifice to build an estate,
then find they hate you, pray for your death, and shun you
    like a beggar trespassing.

361–62 Revenge

A man's heart shrinks with great suffering,
    Cyrnus, but revenge restores it.

363–64 How to Treat Enemies

Flatter your enemy until he is under your power,
    then punish him with no explanation.

425–28 The Best Fate

Best for human beings is never being born
    or seeing the sunlight's glare;
next is quickly passing Hades' gates
    and lying deep in the ground.

457–60 Don't Marry a Younger Woman

An elderly man should avoid a younger bride
    like a boat that is hard to control;
she slips her anchor, breaks her mooring, and lies up
    by night in strange harbors.

523–24 Wealth Is Not Judgmental

Men honor you justly, Wealth; you are
    so tolerant of human vice!

527–28 Double Trouble

I hate both youth and ruinous age: one
    for coming, the other for leaving.

535–38 Slaves Naturally Inferior

No slave is born with an upright head; his neck
    is always crooked and bowed.
Neither rose nor hyacinth blooms from a weed; no noble
    child is born of a slave.

539–40 The Author of the Above Could Be Enslaved

Unless the gods deceive me, Cyrnus, this man
    is forging chains for himself.

567–70 Enjoy Youth while You Can

I play, enjoying my youth. When I die, I will lie
    in the earth for a long time

stone-dumb. Though virtuous, I will leave the light and never
    see anything again.

575–76 He Can't Trust Anybody

I sail around my enemy, like a pilot avoiding
    a reef; so my friends betray me.

619–20 Financial Shipwreck

I roll distraught in waves of desperation; we failed
    to round Cape Poverty.

621–22 All Honor Wealth

This is the one universal law: honor
    the rich and despise the poor.

655–56 Blunt Condolence

All of us share in your sorrow, Cyrnus, but grief
    for another passes quickly.

783–88 No Place Like Home

Once I traveled to Sicily's land, once
    to Euboea's vine-rich plain
and Sparta, glorious city on the reedy Eurotas.
    The people I met greeted me
kindly, but gave my heart no pleasure. Nothing
    is dearer than one's own home.

847–50 People Ready For Slavery

Kick these brainless commoners! Sting them with goads!
    Make them feel the yoke!
Of all the men under the sun you will never
    find a group more servile.

1069–70 Old Age as Sad as Death

Fools and children lament the dead but not
    the wilted bloom of youth.

1135–46 Hope Is All We Have

Hope is the only divinity left among men.
    The others returned to Olympus.
Faith, a great goddess, and Moderation are gone.
    The Graces abandoned the earth.
Just, reliable Oaths are not to be found.
    No one reveres the gods.
God-fearing men are extinct. People know
    no laws or acts of piety.
But as long as life and sunlight last, a man
    should worship Hope above all.
He should pray to the others, but burning thighbones, sacrifice
    first and last to Hope.

1185–86 Brain And Tongue Rarely Go Together

Wisdom and eloquence are a good combination, but rare
    is the man who dispenses them both.

1197–1202 Dispossessed Landowner's Complaint

Son of Polypas, I heard the shrill bird
    whose arrival signals the time
for ploughing, and it jolted my gloomy heart, since others
    possess my flowery fields
and no mules pull a curved plowshare for me . . .[4]

1255–56 Keys to Happiness

A man with no love for youths, horses, or dogs
    never enjoys himself.

1259–62 Criticism of His Boyfriend

Your form is fair, my boy, but a great wreath
    of stupidity encircles your head.
Like a hawk, you suddenly change direction, seduced
    by the words of other men.

1299–1304 Appeal to His Boyfriend

How long will you flee my eager pursuit, my boy?
    Just let me reach the end
of disdain. It is greedy and stubborn to run away!
    You are as cruel as a hawk!

Stop! Be kind! You will not have the gift
  of violet-crowned Aphrodite for long.

1345–50 Defense of Pederasty

Pederasty has been a joy ever since the king
  of immortals, loving Ganymede,
snatched him off to Olympus and made him a god
  in the lovely bloom of youth.
Do not be surprised, Simonides, if I am also
  overcome by a beautiful boy.

Appendices

Appendix 1: Sources of Fragments

Archilochus

1. Cologne Papyrus 58.3–35
2. Ibid., 36–40
3. Oxyrhynchus Papyrus 2310
4. Aristotle, *Eudemian Ethics* 1236A33
5. Heraclitus, *Homeric Allegories* 5
6. Dio Chrysostom 33.17
7. Plutarch, *The E at Delphi* 386D
8. Ibid., *Exile* 604C
9. Ibid., *Galba* 27.9
10. Ibid., *How to Study Poetry* 33AB
11. Ibid., *Peace of Mind* 470BC
12. Ibid., *Ancient Customs of the Spartans* 239B
13. Ibid., *Theseus* 5.2–3
14. Galen, *Hippocrates' Essay on Limbs* 18(1).604
15. Hephaestion, *Handbook* 15.9
16. Theophilus of Antioch, *To Autolycus* 2.37
17. Athenaeus 30F
18. Ibid., 76B
19. Ibid., 299A
20. Ibid., 433E
21. Ibid., 447B
22. Ibid., 483D
23. Ibid., 627C
24. Ibid., 628A
25. Orion of Thebes, *Etymologicum* 55.22
26. Stobaeus 1.1.18
27. Ibid., 3.20.28
28. Ibid., 4.20.43
29. Ibid., 4.20.45
30. Ibid., 4.41.24
31. Ibid., 4.46.10
32. Ibid., 4.56.30
33. Ibid., 4.58.4
34. *Etymologicum Gudianum* s.v. *atrygetos*
35. Scholion on Euripides, *Medea* 679
36. Scholion on Hermogenes, *Rhet. Gr.* 7.820.17

Semonides

1.	Stobaeus 2.1.10
2.	Ibid., 4.22.193
3.	Ibid., 4.34.15
4.	Ibid., 4.53.2
5.	Ibid., 4.56.4

Callinus

1.	Stobaeus 4.10.12

Mimnermus

1.	Athenaeus 469F-70B
2.	Stobaeus 3.7.11
3.	Ibid., 3.11.2
4.	Ibid., 4.20.16
5.	Ibid., 4.34.12
6.	Ibid., 4.50.32
7.	Ibid., 4.50.68
8.	Ibid., 4.50.69 and Theognis 1017–22

Tyrtaeus

1.	Lycurgus, *Against Leocrates* 107
2.	Diodorus Siculus 7.12.6
3.	Strabo 6.3.3
4.	Plutarch, *Lycurgus* 6
5.	Pausanias 4.6.5
6–7.	Ibid., 4.14.5
8.	Stobaeus 4.9.16
9.	Ibid., 4.10.1

Alcman

1.	Oxyrhynchus Papyrus 2387
2.	Louvre Papyrus E 3320
3.	Antigonus of Carystus, *Wonders* 13 (27), p. 8 Keller
4.	Strabo 10.2.22
5.	Apollonius the Sophist, *Homeric Lexicon* s.v. *knodalon*
6.	Hephaestion, *Handbook* 13.6
7–8.	Athenaeus 416CD
9.	Ibid., 498F-499A
10–11.	Ibid., 600F
12–13.	Syrianus, *On Hermogenes' types of style* 1.61.14–21

14.   Stephanus of Byzantium, *Ethnica* s.v. *Erysiche*

Solon

1–2.   Aristotle, *Constitution of the Athenians* 5
3–4.   Ibid., 11.2–12
5–7.   Ibid., 12.3
8.   Demosthenes, *On the embassy* 254 ff.
9.   Philo, *On the creation* 104
10–11. Plutarch, *Solon* 2.3
12.   Ibid., 3.2
13.   Ibid., 3.6
14–15. Ibid., 14.8–9
16–17. Ibid., "Dialogue on Love," 751B–E
18.   Clement of Alexandria, *Miscellanies* 5.81.1
19.   Ibid., 5.129.5
20–21. Diogenes Laertius 1.47
22–24. Ibid., 1.49–51
25.   Stobaeus 3.9.23
26.   Ibid., 4.34.23.

Alcaeus

1.   Oxyrhynchus Papyrus 1789 and Heraclitus, *Homeric Allegories* 5
2.   Ibid., 2302 and Cologne Papyrus 2021
3–6.   Ibid., 1233
7–8.   Ibid., 2165
9.   Heraclitus, *Homeric Allegories* 5
10–17. Athenaeus 429F–430D
18.   Ibid., 627AB
19.   John Tzetzes, *Commentary on Lycophron* 212

Sappho

1.   Inscription edited by Norsa, *Annali di R. Scuola n.s. di Pisa*, ser. 2, vol. 6, 1937, fasc. 1–2, 8 ff.
2.   Copenhagen Papyrus 301 and Milan Papyrus 32
3.   Oxyrhynchus Papyrus 7
4.   Ibid., 1232
5.   Ibid., 1231
6.   Berlin Papyrus 9722
7.   Aristotle, *Rhetoric* 1367E
8.   Dionysius of Halicarnassus, *On composition* 23
9.   Tryphon, *Figures of Speech* 25
10.   Demetrius, *On style* 106
11.   Ibid., 140
12.   Ibid., 141
13.   Ibid., 146

14.	Ibid., 148
15.	Ibid., 162
16.	"Longinus," *On the sublime* 10
17–18.	Hephaestion, *Handbook* 7.6
19–21.	Ibid., 7.7
22.	Ibid., 10.4
23.	Ibid., 10.5
24.	Ibid., 11.2
25–27.	Ibid., 11.5
28.	Ibid., 15.18
29.	Ibid., 15.26
30.	Athenaeus 21BC
31.	Ibid., 674C-E
32–39.	Maximus of Tyre 18.9
40.	Stobaeus 3.4.12
41.	Ibid., 4.22.112
42.	Syrianus, *Commentary on Hermogenes' Types of Style* 1.1
43.	Eustathius, *Commentary on the Iliad* 8.555

Stesichorus

1.	Lille Papyrus 76
2.	Oxyrhynchus Papyrus 2617
3.	Plato, *Phaedrus* 243A
4.	Plutarch, "Slowness of Divine Vengeance" 555A
5.	Athenaeus 81D
6.	Ibid., 469E
7.	Scholion on Euripides, *Orestes* 249

Ibycus

1.	Oxyrhynchus Papyri 1790 and 2081
2.	Plutarch, *Convivial Questions* 9.15.2
3.	Athenaeus 57F–58A
4.	Ibid., 601B
5.	Proclus on Plato, *Parmenides* 137A

Phocylides

1.	Aristotle, *Politics* 1295B.28
2.	Strabo 10.5.12
3.	Dio Chrysostom 36.12–13
4.	Stobaeus 2.15.8
5.	Ibid., 4.15.6
6.	Ibid., 4.22.192
7.	Ibid., 4.29.28
8.	Orion of Thebes, *Anthology* 1.22
9.	Scholion on Aristophanes, *Clouds* 240

Hipponax

1.   Italian Pap. Soc. Papyrus 1089
2.   Strasbourg Papyrus 3
3.   Erotian, *Hippocratic Lexicon* s.v. *ambidexios*
4.   Hephaestion, *Handbook* 5.3
5.   Athenaeus 304B
6.   Ibid., 698B
7.   Stobaeus 4.22.35
8.   *Suda* s.v. *Bupalus*
9–14. John Tzetzes, *Chiliades* 5.728–59
15.   Ibid., *Commentary on Lycophron* 425
16–17. Ibid., 855
18.   Ibid., *Commentary on Aristophanes, Wealth* 87

Xenophanes

1.   Herodian the Grammarian, *Anomalous Words* 41.5
2.   Athenaeus 54E
3.   Ibid., 413F-414C
4.   Ibid., 462C-F
5.   Ibid., 526AB
6.   Sextus Empiricus, *Against the Logicians* 1.49
7.   Ibid., *Against the Physicists* 1.144
8.   Ibid., 1.193
9–11. Clement of Alexandria, *Miscellanies* 5.109
12.   Ibid., 7.22
13–14. Diogenes Laertius 8.36
15.   Ibid., 9.18–19
16.   Stobaeus 1.8.2
17–18. Simplicius, *Commentary on Aristotle's Physics* 23.9–20
19.   Scholion on the *Iliad* 11.27

Anacreon

1.   Heraclitus, *Homeric Allegories* 5
2.   Strabo 3.2.14
3.   Dio Chrysostom 2.62
4.   Hephaestion, *Handbook* 5.2
5.   Ibid., 7.2
6.   Ibid., 10.4
7–8.   Ibid., 12.4
9.   Ibid., 12.5
10.   Ibid., 15.10
11.   Ibid., *Concerning Poems* 4.8
12.   Ibid., 7.2
13.   Aelianus, *On the characteristics of animals* 7.39
14–15. Athenaeus 427AB

16.   Ibid., 433F
17.   Ibid., 463A
18.   Ibid., 782A
19–20. Ibid., 533E-534A
21.   Ibid., 564D
22.   Ibid., 599CD
23.   Stobaeus 4.51.12
24.   *Palatine Anthology* 7.226
25.   Ibid., 13.4
26.   Herodian, *Figures of Speech* 8.599
27.   Scholion on Aristophanes, *Birds* 1372
28.   Ibid., Euripides, *Hecuba* 934
29.   Ibid., *Iliad* 15.192
30.   Ibid., *Iliad* 23.88
31.   Ibid., Pindar, *Olympian* 7.5
32.   Ibid., Pindar, *Isthmian* 2.13

Simonides

1–3.   Herodotus 7.228
4.   Thucydides 6.59.3
5–13.   Plato, *Protagoras* 339A–346E
14.   Aristotle, *Rhetoric* 1405B
15.   Diodorus Siculus 11.11
16.   Dionysus of Halicarnassus, *On composition* 26
17.   Plutarch, *Consolation to Apollonius* 11
18.   Ibid., 17
19.   Ibid., *Old Men in Public Affairs* 1
20.   Ibid., *The Malice of Herodotus* 42
21.   Aelius Aristides 28.60
22.   Hephaestion, *Handbook* 28
23.   Pollux, *Onomasticon* 5.47
24.   Theophilus of Antioch, *To Autolycus* 2.8
25.   Ibid., 2.37
26.   Athenaeus 512C
27.   Clement of Alexandria, *Miscellanies* 4.7.48
28.   Diogenes Laertius 1.89–90
29.   Stobaeus 1.8.15
30.   Ibid., 1.8.22
31.   Ibid., 4.34.14
32.   Ibid., 4.34.28
33.   Ibid., 4.41.9
34.   Ibid., 4.51.5
35.   *Palatine Anthology* 10.105
36.   Ibid., 10.415
37.   Scholion on Aristophanes, *Peace* 736

Corinna

1–2. Berlin Papyrus 284

Appendix 2: Concordance with Standard Editions

A. Archilochus, Semonides, Mimnermus, Tyrtaeus, Solon, Hipponax: M = Mulroy; D = Diehl; W = West

Archilochus

M	D	W	M	D	W	M	D	W
1	*	196a	13	3	3	25	9	14
2	*	188	14	60	114	26	68	131
3	*	23.8–21	15	118	196	27	67a	128
4	13	15	16	66	126	28	102	191
5	56	105	17	2	2	29	104	193
6	60	114	18	53	116	30	58	130
7	71	118	19	115	189	31	74	122.1–9
8	18	21	20	69	125	32	7	13
9	61	101	21	28	42	33	64	133
10	10.3–4	11	22	5.6–9	4.6–9	34	102	cp. 43
11	22	19	23	1	1	35	72	119
12	6	5	24	77	120	36	88	172

Semonides

M	D	W	M	D	W	M	D	W
1	27	42	3	1	1	5	2	2
2	7	7	4	3	3			

Mimnermus

M	D	W	M	D	W	M	D	W
1	10	12	4	1	1	7	4	4
2	13	14	5	2	2	8	5	5
3	8	8	6	3	3			

Tyrtaeus

M	D	W	M	D	W	M	D	W
1	6–7	10	4	3b	4.1–6	7	5.4–5	7
2	3a	4	5	4.1–2	5.1–2	8	8	11
3	4.4–8	5.4–8	6	5.1–3	6	9	9	12

Solon

M	D	W	M	D	W	M	D	W
1	4.1-3	4a	10	14.1-6	24.1-6	19	17	17
2	4.5-8	4c	11	1.7-8	13.7-8	20	2.3-6	2
3	5.1-6	5	12	4.9-12	15	21	2.7-8	3
4	5.7-10	6	13	cp.	10	cp.	9	22
9	10	5	23.13-21	34	14	23.8-12	32	23
10.1-4	9.1-4	6	24	36	15	23.1-7	33	24
8	11	7	25	37	16	12	25	25
1	13	8	3	4	17	20	26	26
15	14	9	19	27	18	16	16	

Hipponax

M	D	W	M	D	W	M	D	W
1	14a	92	6	77	128	15	45	28
2[1]	*	115	7[2]	*	68	16	25	34
3	70.2	121	8	70.1	120	17	24a	32
4	79	119	9-14	6-11	5-10	18	29	36
5	39	26						

Phocylides[3]

M	D	M	D	M	D
1	12	4	11	7	3
2	1	5	7	8	8
3	4	6	2	9	6

B. Xenophanes: D = Diehl, Ds = Diels.

M	D	Ds	M	D	Ds	M	D	Ds
1	34	38	8	10	11	15	7	8
2	18	22	9	19	23	16	16	18
3	2	2	10	12	14	17	22	26
4	1	1	11	13	15	18	21	25
5	3	3	12	14	16	19	28	32
6	30	34	13	6.1	7.1			
7	20	24	14	6.2-5	7.2-5			

1. = Diehl Archilochus 79a.
2. = Diehl *Choliambica Adespota* 1.
3. Not edited by West.

C. Alcaeus and Sappho: V = Voigt, whose numbers correspond to the cumulative numbers in Lobel and Page, except as noted.

Alcaeus

M	V	M	V	M	V	M	V
1	6.1–14	6	34	11	338	16	342
2	298.4–23	7	129.1–24	12	347.1–2	17	346
3	38a	8	130b	13	367.2–3	18	140
4	42	9	208.1–9[1]	14	335	19	333
5	45	10	346.4	15	332		

Sappho

M	V	M	V	M	V	M	V
1	2	11	114	22	140	33	49.2
2	98a + b1–3	12	104a	23	102	34	159
3	5.1–7	13	106	24	154	35	130.2
4	44	14	111	25	82a	36	172
5	16.1–20	15	156	26	91	37	188
6a	94.1–23	16	31.1–16	27	168b	38	47
6b	95.8–13	17	115	28	132	39	150
6c	96.3–17	18	110	29	112.1–2	40	55
7	137	19	49	30	57	41	121
8	1	20	130.1–2	31	81.4–7	42	105a
9	146	21	130.3–4[2]	32	155	43	34
10	105b						

1. = LP 326.
2. = LP 131.

D. Alcman, Stesichorus, Ibycus, Anacreon, Corinna: P = Page, *Poetae Melici Graeci*.

Alcman

M	P	M	P	M	P	M	P
1	3.61–68	5	89	9	56	13	14a
2	1.36–101	6	58	10	59a	14	16.1–4
3	26	7	17	11	59b	4	16.4–5
8	20	12	27				

Stesichorus

M	P	M	P	M	P	M	P
1[1]	*	3	192	5	187	7	223
2[2]	*	4	219	6	185		

Ibycus

M	P	M	P	M	P	M	P
1[3]	*	3	285	5	287	2	310
4	286						

Anacreon

M	P	M	P	M	P	M	P
1	417	9	400	17[4]	*	25	419
2	361	10	393	18	396	26	359
3	357	11	348	19	372	27	378
4	428	12	376	20	388	28	399
5	394b	13	408	21	360	29	362
6	373	14	356a	22	358	30	398
7	413	15	356b	23	395	31	407
8	411	16	389	24[5]	*	32	384

Corinna

1	654 col. i.12–34	2	654 col. iii.12–51

1. Bremer, p. 132, ll. 201–33.
2. Page, *Supplementum* 15.6–17.
3. Ibid., 151.
4. Edmonds 116.
5. Edmonds 149.

E. Simonides: E = Edmonds; P = Page, *Poetae Melici Graeci,* which does not include elegiac poetry attributed to Simonides.

M	E	P	M	E	P	M	E	P
1	118	*	19	95	*	29	199	*
2	119	*	20	92	*	30	200	*
3	120	*	21	175	*	31	26	523
4	139	*	22	160	*	32	97	*
5–13	19	542	23	159	*	33	22	521
14	46	515	24	32	526	34	28	522
15	21	531	25	33	527	35	150	*
16	27	543	26	71	584	36	110	*
17	29	520	27	65	579	37	89	*
18	98	648	28	31	581			

Appendix 3:
Periods and Genres of the Authors Who Quote the Poets

(Where no edition is cited, text and translation are available in the Loeb Classical Library published in Cambridge, Mass., by the Harvard University Press. Texts and translations of the most of the fragments of the lyric poets together with the contexts in which quotations of them are embedded have also been published in the Loeb series; see Edmonds [1928, 1931] and Campbell [*Greek Lyric I* 1982, and *Greek Lyric II* 1989] in the bibliography at the back of this volume.)

1. Aelianus (ca. A.D. 170–235) taught rhetoric at Rome. Surviving works are collections of anecdotes, *On the Characteristics of Animals* and *Miscellaneous History*. Source of Anacreon 13, implying that does have antlers.

2. Antigonus of Carystus (fl. 240 B.C.), an author of miscellaneous works including character sketches and art history. Only *Wonders* survives, a collection of hard-to-believe anecdotes. Source of Alcman's wish to be a kingfisher [3], which Antigonus misinterprets as supporting an improbable theory. Edited by O. Keller in *Rerum Naturalium Scriptores Graeci Minores* I (Leipzig: Teubner, 1877).

3. Apollonius the Sophist (ca. A.D. 100), known only as the author of a Homeric lexicon, which has been abridged. Source of Alcman 5. Edited by I. Bekker (Berlin: Reimer, 1833).

4 Aristides, Aelius (A.D. 117/129–189), famous orator. Fifty-five of his speeches survive, exemplifying the height of eloquence in their day. The source of Simonides 21. Edited by B. Keil (Berlin: Weidmann, 1898).

5. Aristotle (384–322 B.C.), the famous philosopher, pupil of Plato and tutor of Alexander the Great. Numerous essays survive, which are technical in style. An essay, *Constitution of the Athenians*, is one of the chief sources of our information about Solon [2–7]. Elsewhere he provides interesting quotations from Archilochus [4], Sappho [7], Phocylides [1], and Simonides [14].

6. Athenaeus (fl. ca. A.D. 200), see Introduction, pp. 17–18.

7. Clement of Alexandria (ca. A.D. 150–211/216), head of catechetical school at Alexandria, instructing converts to Christianity, around A.D. 200. His surviving works include *Miscellanies* in eight books, subordinating Greek to Christian philosophy. He was well versed in Greek literature, and is the source of Solon 18–19, Xenophanes 9–12, and Simonides 27. *Miscellanies* 1–6 edited by L. Fruechtel (Berlin: Akademie Verlag, 1960).

8. Demetrius (1st cent. A.D.?) author of an impressive essay, "On style," which preserves a number of Sappho's colorful lines [10–15].

9. Demosthenes (384–322 B.C.), the most famous Athenian orator. In legend, he trained by haranguing the waves with pebbles in his mouth. His public life was devoted to futile opposition to the rising power of Macedonia. Numerous political and legal speeches survive. The source of Solon's long fragment 8.

10. Dio Cocceianus, later "Chrysostom" (golden-mouthed) (ca. A.D. 40 to at least A.D. 112), orator and philosopher. Eighty speeches survive. He gained fame as an orator by preaching the adoption of a philosophical lifestyle with the zeal of a modern evangelist. The source of Archilochus 6, Phocylides 3, and Anacreon 3.

11. Diodorus Siculus (wrote ca. 60–30 B.C.; died after 21 B.C.), the author of a *History* in forty volumes, a compilation of others' works. Fifteen volumes are fully preserved; others survive in fragments. Source of historically significant fragments by Tyrtaeus [2] and Simonides [15].

12. Diogenes Laertius (3rd cent. A.D.?), author of "Lives of the Philosophers," a loose compilation, important because it is the only work of its kind to survive. The source of Solon 20–24, Xenophanes 13–15, and Simonides 28.

13. Dionysius of Halicarnassus (wrote 30–8 B.C.), literary critic and historian. His insightful essay on the arrangement of words, *On composition*, is the source of two famous fragments, Sappho 8 and Simonides 16. His twenty-volume history, *Roman Antiquities*, goes from the foundation of Rome to the First Punic War.

14. Erotian (1st cent. A.D.), grammarian and doctor of the Neronian age, author of a glossary to the medical writings of Hippocrates. The source of Hipponax 3, in which the poet boasts of being ambidextrous. Edited by E. Nachmanson (Uppsala: Appelberg, 1918).

15. *Etymologicum Gudianum*, an etymological dictionary compiled about A.D. 1100. Source of Archilochus 34. Edited by A. de Stefani (Leipzig: Teubner, 1909).

16. Eustathius (d. ca. A.D. 1194), a leading scholar of his day. He was archbishop of Thessalonica from 1175 until his death. Author of treatises and letters on contemporary issues and of commentaries on classical literature, especially *Commentaries on Homer's Iliad and Odyssey*, which are the source of Sappho 43. Edited by M. van der Valk (Leiden: Brill, 1971).

17. Galen (A.D. 129?—199), court physician of Marcus Aurelius. Prolific writer and major influence on later generations; source of Archilochus 14. Edited by C. G. Kuehn (Leipzig: Cnoblochius, 1821–33).

18. Hephaestion (2nd cent. A.D.), see Introduction, p. 17. Hephaestion's *Handbook* with appendices and scholia is edited by M. Consbruch (Stuttgart: Teubner, 1971). An English translation of the handbook with commentary exists: J.M. van Ophuijesen, *Hephaestion on Meter* (Leiden: Brill, 1987).

19. Heraclitus (1st cent. A.D.?) not to be confused with the famous early Greek philosopher of the same name. This Heraclitus is the author of a

treatise entitled *Homeric Allegories*. The first chapter gives a general definition of allegory and examples from Archilochus [5], Alcaeus [9], and Anacreon [1]. Edited by E. Mehler (Leiden: Brill, 1851).

20. Herodian the Grammarian (2nd cent. A.D.), son of a distinguished grammarian, Apollonius Dyscolus. Active during the reign of Marcus Aurelius (161–180 A.D.). A prolific writer; extensive excerpts and two complete works survive: a short lexicon and a treatise, *Anomalous Words*. The latter is the source of Xenophanes 1. It is edited by A. Lentz in *Grammatici Graeci* 3.2 (Leipzig: Teubner, 1868).

21. Herodian the Rhetorician, known only as the author of a short treatise, *On figures of speech*, of uncertain date. The source of Anacreon 26. Edited by L. Spengel in *Rhetores Graeci* (Leipzig: Teubner, 1853–56).

22. Herodotus (ca. 500–ca. 430 B.C.), author of the classic *History of the Persian Wars*. Source of epitaphs for the dead at Thermopylae, attributed by some to Simonides [1–3].

23. "Longinus" (fl. A.D. 80?), the name traditionally given to the unknown author of the essay *On the sublime*," one of the best examples of ancient literary criticism. The source of Sappho 16.

24. Lycurgus (d. 324 B.C.), Athenian orator and ally of Demosthenes. A severe public prosecutor. *Against Leocrates* (ca. 332) is his only surviving speech. It is the source of a long excerpt from Tyrtaeus [1].

25. Maximus of Tyre (ca. A.D. 125–185), author of forty-one extant lectures. An avid follower of Plato, whom he frequently quotes. The source of Sappho 32–39, brief excerpts by which she is made to seem a "Socratic" lover. In the sequel, Maximus applies the same reasoning to Anacreon. Edited by H. Hobein (Leipzig: Teubner, 1910).

26. Orion of Thebes, known only as the author of two extant works of uncertain date: a brief (eighteen-page) anthology, which contains mostly excerpts of Euripides, and an etymological dictionary. The anthology is the source of Phocylides 8 and is edited by A. Meineke in *Ioannis Stobaei Florilegium* IV (Leipzig: Teubner, 1857). The dictionary is the source of Archilochus 25 and is edited by F.G. Sturz (Leipzig: Weigel, 1820).

27. *Palatine Anthology*, a collection of Greek poems in fifteen volumes compiled from previous anthologies under Emperor Constantine VII (A.D. 912–959) by a scholar named Cephalas. The only known manuscript of the anthology was found in the Heidelberg library of Count Palatine. The collection contains many apparently false attributions to the early lyric poets, but may preserve some genuine works. Anacreon 24–25 and Simonides 35–36 are given as interesting examples of these doubtful attributions.

28. Papyri, see Introduction, pp. 15–16.

29. Pausanias (fl. ca. A.D. 150), geographer. Author of the valuable *Description of Greece* in ten books. Source of Tyrtaeus 5–7.

30. Philo (30 B.C.–A.D. 45), theologian and head of the Jewish community in Alexander. Numerous essays survive in which he attempts to demonstrate similarity between Jewish and Greek beliefs. Source of Solon's poem on the ages of man [9].

31. Plato (ca. 429–347 B.C.), the famous Athenian philosopher. His writings are in the form of dialogues, in which Socrates plays the leading role. The source of the beginning of Stesichorus' palinode [3] and a summary of and excerpts from a long poem by Simonides on virtue [5–13].

32. Plutarch (ca. A.D. 46–at least 120), see Introduction, p. 16.

33. Pollux, Julius (2nd cent. A.D.), scholar and rhetorician. His *Onomasticon* survives in abridged form. It is a kind of thesaurus, containing surveys of vocabulary relevant to various topics with occasional citations sometimes added. The source of Simonides 23, an epitaph for a dog, which follows Pollux' list of different kinds of dogs. Edited by E. Bethe in *Lexicographi Graeci* 9 (Stuttgart: Teubner, 1967).

34. Proclus (ca. A.D. 410–484), a leading Neoplatonic philosopher. Author of hymns combining ancient polytheism with Platonic philosophy, also numerous commentaries on Plato and other philosophical works. His commentary on Plato's *Parmenides* is the source of Ibycus' poem comparing himself to a race horse [5]. Edited with French translation by A.E. Chaignet (Frankfurt am Main: Minerva, 1900–1903).

35. Scholia. For most ancient authors, the oldest extant manuscripts were written in the Middle Ages. They descend from ancient editions, being copies of copies etc., going back to the works of Hellenistic scholars, who produced the first scholarly editions. Most manuscripts have marginal notes, known as scholia, which have been collected, edited, and published separately in modern times. The value of scholia is uneven, since they may derive from the earliest Hellenistic scholars, the manuscript's latest copiest, or any point between. Fragments of lost works occur in scholia. Scholia to the *Iliad*, edited by H. Erbse (Berlin: De Gruyter, 1969) are the source of Xenophanes 19, and Anacreon 29 and 30. Pindar scholia, edited by A.B. Drachmann (Leipzig: Teubner, 1903), account for Anacreon 31 and 32; Euripides scholia, edited by E. Schwartz (Berlin: Reimer, 1887–91), for Archilochus 35, Stesichorus 7, and Anacreon 28. Scholia to Aristophanes, edited by Fr. Dübner (Paris: Firmin-Didot, 1877), are the source of Phocylides 9, Anacreon 27, and Simonides 37. Hermogenes scholia, edited by C. Walz in *Rhetores Graeci* 7 (Stuttgart: J.G. Cotta 1832–36), are the source for Archilochus 36.

36. Sextus Empiricus (late 2nd cent. A.D.) physician and skeptical philosopher. Only his philosophical works survive, which outline the doctrines of the skeptical school of philosophy. The source of Xenophanes 6–8.

37. Simplicius (6th cent. A.D.) wrote commentaries on works of Aristotle. His commentary on Aristotle's *Physics* is the source of two of Xenophanes' theological fragments [17–18]. It is edited by H. Diels in *Commentaria in Aristotelem Graeca* 9, 10 (Berlin: Reimer, 1882–1909)

38. Stephanus of Byzantium (5th cent. A.D.), the author of the *Ethnica*, a geographical dictionary, of which a few original articles and numerous excerpts survive. The source of Alcman 14, which lies behind the theory that he was Lydian. Edited by A. Meineke (Berlin: Reimer, 1849).

39. Stobaeus, Johannes (5th cent. A.D.) see Introduction, p. 18. Edited by Wachsmuth and Hense (Berlin: Weidmann, 1884–1912).

40. Strabo (64/3 B.C.–A.D. 21 at least), historian and geographer. His *Geography* in seventeen volumes survives. The source of quotations from Tyrtaeus [3], Alcman [4], Phocylides [2], and Anacreon [2].

41. *Suda* (ca. A.D. 1000), the name of a lexicon, from medieval Latin meaning "Fortress." A compilation of scholia and commentaries of uneven quality, important for the preservation of excerpts of early Greek scholarship. Source of Hipponax 8. Edited by A. Adler in *Lexicographi Graeci* 1.1–5 (Leipzig: Teubner 1929–38).

42. Syrianus (5th cent. A.D.), Athenian scholar, one of Proclus' (q.v.) teachers. Author of surviving commentaries on Aristotle's *Metaphysics* and Hermogenes' *Types of Style*, an influential second-century treatise. The latter commentary is the source of Alcman 12–13 and Sappho 42. Syrianus' *In Hermogenem* is edited by H. Rabe (Leipzig: Teubner, 1892–99) as are the works of Hermogenes himself, in *Rhetores Graeci* 6 (Leipzig: Teubner, 1913). Hermogenes' *Types of Style* has been translated into English by C.W. Wooten (Chapel Hill: University of North Carolina Press, 1987).

43. Theophilus of Antioch (2nd cent. A.D.), bishop of Antioch in 169. His surviving work, *To Autolycus*, is designed to convert pagans to Christianity. He is the source of Archilochus 16 and Simonides 24–25. There is a text and English translation by R.M. Grant (London: Oxford University Press, 1970).

44. Thucydides (5th cent. B.C.), author of the history of the Peloponnesian War between Athens and Sparta; source of Simonides 4.

45. Tryphon (1st cent. B.C.), an important grammarian. A short treatise, *Figures of Speech*, is completely preserved; this is the source of a proverb either invented or quoted by Sappho [9]. Edited by Spengel in *Rhetores Graeci* 3 (Leipzig: Teubner, 1856).

46. Tzetzes, John (12th cent. A.D.), a colorful Byzantine scholar. The author of commentaries on Homer, Hesiod, Aristophanes, and Lycophron, the last a proverbially obscure poet. Tzetzes also wrote voluminous versified works. The largest, usually called *Chiliades (Thousands)*, is 12,674 lines long and is a commentary on Tzetzes' own letters. It is the source of Hipponax' verses on the *pharmakos* ritual [9–14]. The *Chiliades* is edited under the more formal title, *Historiae*, by P.A.M. Leone (Naples: Libreria scientifica editrice, 1968). Tzetzes' account of the ritual, lacking corroboration, must be taken with a grain of salt, since he was an unreliable scholar. His other commentaries preserve Hipponax 15–18 and Alcaeus 19. His commentary on Lycophron is edited by G. Miller (Leipzig: Vogel, 1811); his commentaries on Aristophanes by L. Massa Positano, D. Holwerda, and W.J.W. Koster (Groningen: J.B. Wolters, 1960–).

Notes

Introduction

1. Hammond 690 gives 1220 as the date for the first raids, 1200 for the fall of Troy, and 1120 for the final collapse of Mycenae.

2. The recent excavation of a rare Dark Age settlement has stirred interest. The site is Lefkandi (ancient name unknown), located on the island of Euboea where it comes closest to the mainland. Lefkandi was probably a major settlement in its area, even an international crossroads, since excavators have found evidence of trade with Cyprus there. According to Snodgrass 18, on the basis of the community's burials, its entire population numbered approximately twenty-five early in the ninth century B.C.

3. For a more complete description of the invention see Havelock 77–88.

4. For a recent survey of the problem of dating the invention of the alphabet, see Isserlin.

5. Proposed by Wade-Gery 11–14, recently defended as a viable hypothesis by Powell.

6. Evidence is provided by the archaeological site of Al Mina, on the Syrian coast at the mouth of the Orontes River opposite Cyprus, the edge of the Assyrian empire. Here Greeks from Euboea and Cyprus traded with the Assyrians. Al Mina was discovered and excavated by Sir Leonard Woolley in the 1930s, who deduced from geographical and historical factors that a trading center had existed on the site. On the historical significance of Al Mina, see S. Smith's article. Smith described his essay as a "trial balloon," but it is still cited.

7. Cook (1975) 800.

8. Cook (1958) 22–23.

9. Graham 160–62 lists 139 known colonies. Almost all are coastal: thirty-six in southern Italy and Sicily, forty-three in the Black Sea and the Hellespont, and thirty-three in the northern Aegean.

10. For the text I used L.H. Jeffery 409 (plate 47).

11. E.g., West 23.

12. A line of iambic "trimeter" consisted of six feet, mostly iambs (short-long), while trochaic "tetrameter" consisted of eight feet, mostly trochees (long-short). In iambic and trochaic verses, different rules applied to even-numbered feet than to odd. Hence metricians described iambic and trochaic verses as consisting of so many *metra* (measures) of two feet (an odd and an

even) each. A line of six iambs had three *metra* and was thus called a trimeter, etc.

13. Budge 2.148–50 (Aristotle) and 345–55 (Bacchylides).

14. A "catalectic" (broken off) verse was one whose last metrical foot was incomplete—a common phenomenon; "acatalectic" means not broken off. As written by Sappho, acatalectic dactylic pentameter had fourteen syllables because the first foot consisted of only two syllables, which could be either long or short. Many Aeolic meters began with two such syllables, which are known as an "Aeolic base." "Logaoedic" means "between speech (*logos*) and song (*aoide*)." Logaoedic dactyls were presumably recited with more musical intonation than normal dactyls. A "trochaic syzygy" is just a pair of trochees. The "Praxilleion" was named after a minor classical poetess, Praxilla.

Translations

Archilochus

1. Scholars cannot agree on whether Archilochus describes full sexual intercourse at the end of the poem. Some believe that he honors his pledge to stop "in the grassy garden." This seems to me like believing that the check really is in the mail, but I have attempted to preserve the ambiguity of the original, such as it is.

2. Aristotle (*Rhetoric* 3.16) uses these lines to illustrate the device of putting negative judgments into the mouths of third parties rather than presenting them as one's own. He says Archilochus attributes this speech to "Charon the carpenter." He also cites fragment 31 as an example of this device.

3. A collection of proverbs by Zenobius (2nd cent. A.D.) preserves a famous proverb that is sometimes attributed to Archilochus: "The fox knows many tricks; the hedgehog, one great one" (5.68). Zenobius does not, however, credit these words to Archilochus. He just says that Archilochus *refers* to the proverb in an epode. It seems likely that fragment 16 contains the Archilochean lines that Zenobius had in mind.

4. Aristotle (*Rhetoric* 3.16) cites the beginning of this with that of fragment 11 (see note 2 above). He says that Archilochus gives these words to a father bewildered by his daughter's behavior.

Semonides

1. The lines are corrupt and may be restored with or without a negative adverb. Those who read the statement as positive, i.e., the woman does draw her chair closer to the fire, think that the idea is that she does *only* that, rather than adding wood as she should. I follow Lloyd-Jones in assuming that the main verb was originally negated: she is so inert that she doesn't even move up to the fire.

2. The meaning of the last sentence is debatable. Literally, it is: "We should not be tormented holding our spirits upon bad pains." I think it

means that we should not cling to our lives on the terms of long suffering, but Campbell's interpretation, that we should not dwell on our troubles, is certainly defensible.

Mimnermus

1. A cryptic utterance, which really consists of only a line and a half of the standard elegiac couplet. Literally, "Let there be truth to you and me, the most just property of all."

2. Lines 1–6 are also transmitted as a separate poem in the *Theognidean Anthology*, lines 1017–22. Only lines 4–8 are actually preserved in Stobaeus, where they are attributed to Mimnermus.

Tyrtaeus

1. According to the Stobaeus manuscripts, Tyrtaeus says that it is *argaleon* (difficult, unpleasant) to cleave the back of a retreating enemy. It seems an odd thing for such a fanatical militarist to say; one editor proposes reading *harpaleon* (pleasurable, enticing) instead. I have stayed with the transmitted text and emphasized a contrast with the following couplet: "Though killing an enemy in retreat is disagreeable, it is better than the alternative: dying in disgrace."

Alcman

1. West (1965).

Solon

1. *Seisachtheia* (shaking the burden) designated Solon's economic reforms. Among surviving sources, Aristotle is the first to use it. In his life of Solon (15.2), however, Plutarch says that Solon himself coined the term as a positive way of describing his controversial economic measures. If so, Solon has the dubious honor of being the first politician in recorded history to utilize euphemism.

2. Literally, "the inescapable wound goes to the whole city." Some scholars feel that it is anachronistic to read the image of a spreading infection into Solon's words, since his term for wound (*helkos*) cannot be demonstrated to have included the notion of infection in pre-Classical Greek. It seems to me, however, that Solon's own words, i.e., his reference to a wound *moving*, make it very likely that he was thinking of what we call an infection.

3. These lines appear in the *Theognidean Anthology* 719–28 and in Stobaeus 4.33.7 (where they are attributed to Theognis) with the following addendum:

That is wealth for men. No one can take
    other possessions to Hades
or use them to buy off death, crushing disease
    or the approach of evil age.

4. This fragment corresponds to lines 7 and 8 from Solon's "Elegy to the Muses," which is quoted in full by Stobaeus, fragment 25.

5. Also in the *Theognidean Anthology* 315–18.

6. Solon's phrase "yearning for thighs and sweet lips" was notorious. It is cited by Athenaeus (602E) together with lines from Aeschylus and Sophocles to illustrate the extent of pederasty in earlier generations. In his *Apology*, Apuleius (2nd cent. A.D.) asks: "Would you deny that Solon was a serious philosopher because he wrote that most lascivious line, 'yearning for thighs and sweet lips'?" Plutarch's quotation from Aeschylus may be from a lost tragedy entitled *The Myrmidons*. If so, the words were probably spoken by Achilles to the dead Patroclus.

7. These lines are also quoted by Diodorus Siculus 9.20.2 with the following addendum:

Landing is difficult when you sail far out; now
     we must carefully weigh all plans.

Alcaeus

1. *Kemelios* is a transliteration of the cult title given to Dionysus. Its meaning is not known.

2. Nothing is known of Onymacles except what can be inferred from this context: he was a proverbial lone wolf.

3. The meter shows that at least two lines have been omitted. This was probably the poem that inspired Horace's Ode I.9, the "Soracte Ode."

4. Proclus on Hesiod *Works and Days* 584 quotes these lines, adding:

but the cricket sounds sweet in the leaves.
The artichoke blooms. Women are at their worst,
and men are feeble, for Sirius is scorching
their head and knees.

The passage is a close imitation of *Works and Days* 582–88.

Sappho

1. There is doubt about the attitude that Sappho expresses towards the departing woman in this passage. To me it seems ironic. I don't think that a person who is genuinely distressed says that she *honestly* wants to die. The fragment is especially intriguing because surviving words raise the possibility, just as the text is becoming fragmentary, that for once Sappho refers unambiguously to sexual contact among her female friends. The adjective in the last line, *apalan*, meaning "tender" or "delicate," is a feminine plural form and usually modifies persons, but it seems hard to believe that Sappho would refer so casually to satisfying one's longing "for delicate young women" (Barnstone 71).

2. A commentary by one Stephanus (7th cent. A.D.) paraphrases the passage as follows:

Either Alcaeus or some other man loved a girl and Sappho depicts their dialogue. The lover says to the beloved, "I want to say something to you, but I hesitate, I am embarrassed, ashamed." The girl replies, "But if you were good and that which you were about to say to me were good, you would not be embarrassed but would speak freely, looking at me without blushing."

The context of these verses is not known. Aristotle could have been thinking of two separate poems, one by Alcaeus with a reply by Sappho, or of a poem by Sappho in which she paraphrases or quotes Alcaeus. Stephanus' statement that the dialogue is between a lover and a beloved may be nothing more than an inference from Aristotle's text, but it is plausible and compatible with Aristotle: Sappho adopts the *persona* of a girl warding off the advances of a seducer created by Alcaeus.

3. Hephaestion, *On poems* 7.1.70, cites the first two lines with an invocation of Hymenaeus, the god of marriage, inserted between phrases, i.e., "Raise the roofbeam (Hymenaeus!) high O carpenters (Hymenaeus!)" etc.

4. Pollux explains the context. This is a wedding hymn. The bride's friends pretend that they would rescue her from the groom but are intimidated by the servant protecting the door.

5. In his metrical Latin handbook on meters, Terentianus Maurus seems to paraphrase this line and its sequel. Sappho uses dactylic pentameter, he writes, *cordi quando fuisse sibi canit Atthida / parvam, florea virginitas sua cum foret* ("When she sings of loving little Atthis, when her maidenhood was still in bloom," lines 154–55; p. 39 Keil). This raises the possibility that fragment 18 above was originally followed by 32: "Once I loved you, Atthis, long ago. / You seemed a small and graceless child."

6. Hephaestion does not name the author of these lines. They are quoted and attributed to Sappho by a late Byzantine scholar, Apostolius (15th cent. A.D.). Modern editors, starting with Wilamowitz, deny the attribution to Sappho because the dialect is not Aeolic.

7. The first two and half lines are quoted by Plutarch, *Precepts on Marriage* 146, with the note that the woman addressed was rich.

Stesichorus

1. Campbell, *Greek Lyric Poetry*, 1982, 254.

2. Lobel (*Oxyrhynchus Papyri* 32, 1) assigned this fragment to Stesichorus' *Geryoneis* on the basis of language and meter and the fact that the name Geryon occurs in a separate fragment of the same sheet (although the initial gamma is missing). The name Geryon is not actually visible in the part of the fragment translated. I have provided it for clarity in line 5; in line 9, remnants of three letters have been conjecturally restored as the beginning of the name.

3. Pleisthenes was one of the ancestors of Agamemnon and Orestes. The snake with bloodied head represents Agamemnon; the Pleisthenid king, Orestes, his avenger.

Ibycus

1. The Molionids were sons of Poseidon and Molione; they once battled Nestor (*Iliad* 11.750) and were eventually killed by Heracles. The notion that they shared a single body appears only in Ibycus' fragment. Ibycus' other details (riding white horses; born from an egg) are usually associated with the Dioscuri, Castor and Polydueces.

Phocylides

1. Everything including Phocylides' signature is included in a single couplet in the Greek; I could not match such conciseness in English.

Hipponax

1. Lines 10 and 11, partially preserved in the papyrus, are cited in their entirety by Tzetzes, *Commentary on the Iliad* 1.273. The scene is similar to Petronius *Satyricon* 138 where a "priestess of Priapus" tries to restore the hero's potency with a similar beating.

Xenophanes

1. Athenaeus quotes the passage from Euripides' lost tragedy the *Autolycus* as follows:

Of all of Greece's countless evils,
none is worse than the tribe of athletes.
They never learn to lead virtuous
lives. How could they? What could a man
enslaved to his jaw, his belly's subject,
ever hope to add to his patrimony?
They cannot deal with need or adapt
to misfortunes. Lacking good habits,
they find it hard to change when they must.
In youth, they are the city's glistening
darlings. When bitter age descends,
they fade from view like tattered coats.
I think our custom is clearly wrong:
holding assemblies on account of athletes,
honoring the useless pleasures they give
at banquets. What has a man who wins
a crown for wrestling well or running
or lofting a discus or smashing a jaw
actually done for his native city?
Do they march into battle against the enemy
with discus in hand? Drive the invader
away by hitting his shield with their fists?

No one facing steel indulges
such foolishness. I think we should crown wise
and virtuous men: the ones who are best
at leading the state with moderation and justice;
the ones whose words prevent the evils
of violent civil strife. Such actions
benefit all of the city and Greece.

Anacreon

1. The Lethaeus was a tributary of the Meander river in southwest Turkey near the city of Magnesia-on-the-Meander. Anacreon refers to a temple of Artemis that stood on its banks. Though founded by Greeks, the city was governed by Persians; it was the site of Polycrates' murder. Hephaestion says that the poem was at the beginning of Anacreon's first book. As it stands, the thought is incomplete; Anacreon must have gone on to make some specific request of Artemis. Hephaestion gives the first three lines of this poem; the rest is quoted by a scholiast.

2. "Leucas' rock" refers to a steep cliff on the island of Leucas off Greece's northwest coast. Disappointed lovers (including Sappho, according to legend) supposedly committed suicide by leaping from it. Anacreon uses the jump as a symbol of "falling" in love.

Simonides

1. The story is told by Thucydides (6.54–59). Hipparchus loved the youth Harmodius but was spurned by him at least in part because he already had an older lover, Aristogeiton. For revenge, Hipparchus invited Harmodius' sister to be a basket-bearer in a religious procession, then had her turned away, saying that she had never been invited and was unworthy. The action drove Harmodius and Aristogeiton to form a conspiracy to kill Hippias and Hipparchus and restore political freedom. The uprising was to take place during the Panathenaea, the festival of Athena. Though their larger plans misfired, Harmodius and Aristogeiton managed to kill Hipparchus. Both of them were caught and executed. Hippias' rule became more oppressive, and he was driven out of Athens in 510 by Athenian nobles in collaboration with the Spartans.

2. Danaë was the daughter of King Acrisius of Argos. Because of an oracle that he would die at his grandson's hands, Acrisius set Danaë and baby Perseus, her son by Zeus, adrift at sea in a wooden chest. They were saved by a fisherman. Perseus grew up to be the hero who beheaded Medusa, saved Andromeda, and founded Mycenae. Late in life, he accidentally killed Acrisius with an errant discus throw.

3. Ephyra is said to be Corinth's ancient name.

4. On the assassination of Hipparchus see note 1 above.

5. The fragment is similar in theme to Semonides 3 and is attributed to him

by some scholars. Certainty is not possible. I have opted for Simonides because the meter is elegiac (otherwise unattested for Semonides), because the poem begins with a quotation (a Simonidean mannerism), and because imagery and transitions seem too smooth for the poet of Amorgos.

Bacchylides

1. Persephone, Demeter's daughter. All of Sicily was considered sacred to Demeter and Persephone.

2. Deinomenes was one of the founders of the Rhodian-Cretan colony of Gela in Sicily. Two of his sons rose through military prowess to become tyrants of neighboring Syracuse: Gelon (485–478), and Hiero (478–467). Under them Syracuse became one of the principal cities of the Mediterranean world. A third son, Thrasybulus, was expelled after a brief reign when Hiero died. Thereafter Syracuse adopted a democratic constitution.

3. Pheres' son = Admetus. Euripides' *Alcestis* preserves the story. King Admetus befriended Apollo, who had to work for him for a year as penance for killing the three Cyclopes. When Apollo learned from the Fates that Admetus was going to die young, he talked them into postponing the king's doom, if he could find a substitute. Admetus' wife, Alcestis, agreed to die instead. On the day she expired, Heracles, another of Admetus' friends, happened to visit his palace. Learning of the events, he wrestled Death into submission and restored Alcestis to life.

4. The meeting of Heracles and Meleager in Hades was probably invented by Bacchylides. Subsequently, Heracles married Deianira after defeating her other leading suitor, a river god, in wrestling.

The story of Heracles' death is preserved in Sophocles' *Women of Trachis*. It involves the poison of the Hydra, a many-headed serpent, which Heracles killed as his second labor. Afterwards, he dipped his arrows in the Hydra's venom, which was the deadliest poison known to myth. Years later, after his marriage to Deianira, Heracles decided to settle in Trachis. En route with Deianira, he came to a swollen river. A centaur, Nessus, offered to ferry Deianira across and she accepted. On the far side, Nessus tried to rape her, but Heracles shot him with one of his poisoned arrows. Feeling the poison in his veins, the dying Nessus told Deianira to save some of his blood because it was an aphrodisiac that would restore Heracles' love, if he ever strayed. She believed him and did so. In time, Heracles fell in love with a young princess, sacked her city, and took her prisoner. To win him back, Deianira sent him a shirt treated with Nessus' blood, but when Heracles put it on, it began eating his flesh. Realizing he was doomed, Heracles lay on a funeral pyre and had himself burned. But his spirit ascended into heaven where he became a god.

5. One of the Muses, later associated with astronomy, but in Bacchylides' day the Muses had not yet acquired their various specialities.

6. See note 2.

7. Because Oeneus neglected to sacrifice to Artemis, she unleashed a giant

boar in his kingdom. Prince Meleager raised an army of heroes to fight it. When the boar was killed, the Calydonians fought over its hide and tusks with a neighboring tribe known as the Curetes, including Meleager's two maternal uncles.

8. The Fates appeared to Meleager's mother, Althaea, shortly after his birth and announced that her son would live only until the log burning in the hearth was consumed by fire. Althaea removed the log from the fire and put it in a chest. Years later, learning that Meleager had killed her brothers, she put the log back in the fire.

Pindar

1. Examples of humor in Pindar's other odes are not difficult to find. In Nemean 1, Pindar depicts the generals of Thebes rushing into baby Heracles' bedroom in full armor to save him from a pair of snakes, only to find that the infant has already strangled them. In Nemean 7 we are told that the son of quick-tempered Achilles met his end in Apollo's temple at Delphi, where he was killed in a quarrel over dividing meat at a sacrificial banquet. In Pythian 3, Zeus kills the healer Asclepius because of the huge fee he charges for restoring the dead. In Pythian 4, Triton, a god who lives on the coast of northern Africa and is therefore lonely, disguises himself as an old man and tries to engage the Argonauts in conversation. As they depart, he casts around for a gift to give them and in desperation hands them a lump of soil. And so forth. This is not to say that Pindar's poetry is never serious. As in most songs, laughter and tears, the ridiculous and the sublime coexist harmoniously in his works.

2. Choral odes generally, including Pindar's, used the Doric dialect. This ode is also "Dorian" because Syracuse was a Dorian colony, founded by Corinth.

3. Clotho, the "Spinner," is one of the Fates. Pindar apparently alludes to a version of the story in which she had a role in reassembling Pelops. Some, e.g., Kirkwood (51), think that Pindar means to say that Pelops was born with an ivory shoulder as a "birthmark," which caused Poseidon to fall in love with him later, but such an interpretation has major difficulties. Gerber (55–56) seems to me to be correct in arguing that at this point Pindar speaks as if he were going to accept the tale of the cannibalistic feast.

4. According to Pindar, Tantalus' punishment was a boulder that dangled menacingly overhead forever. (Would he *never* realize that it was not actually going to fall?)

5. Various interpretations have been proposed. The simplest seems to be that of the scholiast. Tantalus' is one of four famous labors or torments. The others consist of Ixion spinning on his wheel, Sisyphus pushing his rock, and Tityus having his liver eaten by two vultures.

6. "Aeolian" probably refers to the meter of the poem. Viewed rhythmically, Pindar's poems fall into two classes: Aeolic (the type of Olympian 1),

in which the basic unit is the choriamb (—U U—); and dactylo-epitritic in which "epitrites" (—U— —) and dactys (—U U) dominate.

7. Pindar hopes that Hiero's team will eventually win an Olympic chariot race, the most prestigious event. When this finally happened in 468, however, Bacchylides composed the victory ode.

8. The Greek mainland and southern Italy represent Europe, while the Greeks viewed the Turkish coast as part of Asia. By this reckoning, Africa was the third continent to be colonized.

9. Chiron is the wise and virtuous centaur who educated Achilles and Jason. In having Apollo seek Chiron's advice regarding love, Pindar is humanizing him in a humorous way. As a general rule, Apollo gives advice rather than seeks it, and he acts out sexual desires without hesitation. There is no known tradition in which Apollo was Chiron's regular pupil.

10. There is disagreement over the correct interpretation of the exchange between Apollo and Chiron. Here is a literal translation of the passage, beginning with Apollo's final question:

"Is it therefore holy to lay a famous hand on her and to cut sweet grass from / outside of the marriage bed?" The mighty centaur, having laughed warmly with gentle brow, immediately gave his counsel in turn. "The keys of wise Persuasion of sacred loves are hidden and likewise among both gods and men they are ashamed to obtain a pleasurable marriage openly at first. Indeed, kind passion has turned you towards misrepresenting this *logos* [reckoning, explanation, statement, subject], you whom it is not lawful to touch with falsehood."

Woodbury (565) and Carey (76) think that Apollo asks whether he may marry Cyrene. Chiron is amused by his diffidence. He replies, in effect, "Yes, as you know perfectly well, you are destined to take her away to Libya and make her your wife." He says that because of the embarrassment associated with love, Apollo has spoken as if he did not know all this, thus misrepresenting the situation.

This seems to me to be a naive interpretation. Under circumstances like those described, Olympian gods rarely stand on ceremony. Apollo's first impulse would surely be to ravish Cyrene immediately, and that seems the natural way to understand his question whether it would be holy for him to lay his glorious hand upon her, i.e., as a euphemism for rape. Chiron's reply is a mild rebuke, in which he urges Apollo to court Cyrene and marry her properly. That the keys of persuasion are hidden means that it takes a little time to win a maiden's heart. This is the interpretation of Winnington-Ingram, who describes Chiron's words (12) as a sermon "preached lightly and with a humour not always recognised to be characteristic of the poet." It also seems to be supported by Kirkwood (225).

11. Pindar refers to the foundation of Cyrene by colonists from the island of Thera and to its location on a plateau.

12. Aristaeus was a minor god worshipped in Thessaly and in Cyrene. The present passage is one of the principal sources of information about

him. In Vergil's *Georgics* he is the bee-keeper who is chasing Orpheus' wife Eurydice when she is bitten by a poisonous snake.

13. Another controversial passage. Translated literally Pindar says, "Great virtues are always much-mythed, but to *poikillein* [embellish, adorn, embroider] small [things/words] in long [things/words] is hearing for the wise." I think he means that great deeds produce all kinds of stories and it is even entertaining to make elaborate tales out of minor subjects (but one cannot ramble on forever; good timing is of paramount importance). Farnell (205–206) followed by Kirkwood (228) and Carey (88), rejects this interpretation, finding it impossible to believe that Pindar would admit indulging in the lengthy embellishment of minor stories. The interpretation of these men is that producing short works of art in regard to long subjects, i.e., being concise, entertains the wise. This requires taking the verb *poikillein* in the secondary sense of "producing (a work of art)" rather than "adorning (a preexisting thing)" and the preposition *en* (in) in the unusual sense of "concerning."

Although my interpretation is somewhat unusual, it is favored by translators Bowra and Swanson. Pindar certainly did indulge in the lengthy embellishment of minor deeds; an excellent example is the wedding of Alexidamus, with which the present poem ends. That he was capable of ironic statements that—*if taken too seriously*—cast him and his patrons in a bad light should be apparent from the prelude to the second Isthmian ode, where he laments that contemporary poets, obviously including himself, sell their songs for money. In the past, he says, poets only wrote songs for boys whom they really loved. Wilamowitz (264) interpreted the words "to embellish the small in long" in the same way that I do.

14. Pindar digresses to speak of the family of Heracles, who was born in Thebes to Zeus and Alcmena. At the same time that Alcmena delivered Zeus' child, Heracles, she brought forth Iphicles, the son of her human husband, Amphitryon. Iphicles' son Iolaus assisted his uncle Heracles when he performed his famous twelve labors for Eurystheus, the evil king of Mycenae. After the death and deification of Heracles, Eurystheus tried to kill Heracles' children, but the aging Iolaus recovered his youth and slew Eurystheus. Other than illustrating the concept of "doing what the occasion demands" the story has little relevance to the rest of the poem. Pindar's remark that "only the mute would fail to mention Heracles" is a humorous way of explaining why he introduced the tale. He further justifies its inclusion by saying that he prayed to Heracles and Iolaus, presumably for Telesicrates to win a victory. Since they were Theban heroes, it would be logical for Pindar to pray to them.

15. Another disputed passage. I follow Kirkwood (230) in thinking that here Pindar veers back to Telesicrates' athletic career, saying that he (Telesicrates) had previously glorified this city (Cyrene) by winning crowns on the island of Aegina and in the Isthmian Games (near "Nisus' hill").

16. The old man of the sea is probably Nereus, father of the nymphs. The story to which Pindar alludes is not otherwise known.

17. Danaus' fifty daughters had been forced to marry fifty cousins, but all except one murdered her husband on the wedding night. Later another became Poseidon's mistress. The emphasis on the speed and ease with which the forty-eight betrothals were arranged is surely light-hearted. Pindar's audience must have included men chafing under the burden of arranging suitable marriages for one or two daughters.

Corinna

1. Lobel (1930) 356–58.
2. Corinna refers to the Cretan Curetes, demigods who helped Rhea save the infant Zeus from Cronus. They are a different group than the tribe that battled the Calydonians in Bacchylides' fifth victory ode.

Theognidean Anthology

1. What was Theognis' "seal"? It has been interpreted variously as a reference to the vocatives, Cyrnus and Polypaide, to his mention of his own name, and to the quality of his poetry. I think, however, that a suggestion mentioned by Campbell (348–49), that the seal is literal, deserves consideration. A sealed copy of Theognis' poems could actually have provided a check against textual corruption and forgery, assuming that it was preserved and consulted when disagreement arose. It is difficult to see how this could have been done by any feature or quality of the poems themselves. Of course, the command may have been entirely rhetorical: no real seal may have existed. The question is complicated by the fact that whatever the seal was, the poem established the endlessly repeated vocatives "Cyrnus" and "Polypaide" as an indication of Theognidean authorship, a "signature," which resembled a seal except that it could be easily forged by anyone.
2. At least one couplet seems to have dropped out between lines 58 and 59 as they are transmitted. As the text now stands, Theognis says that the "noble" cheat and mock each other.
3. The best of the manuscripts reads *thyme* (O spirit), rather than *Kyrne* (Cyrnus); others give *Kyrne*. I adopt the latter reading, reluctantly disagreeing with both Campbell and West. Campbell (360) cites four other passages in which Theognis addresses his soul. But in each of these Theognis is urging his soul either to be brave or to be happy; he is trying to control his internal state, his private feelings. In such a context, it seems natural to exhort one's spirit. The poem under consideration, however, pertains to superficial behavior. In the last couplet, Theognis refers to changing the color of one's skin to suit the occasion. This is exactly the sort of advice that he addresses to Cyrnus (cp. 61–65). To me it makes no sense as an address to the spirit, which determines how we really feel inside, not how we appear to others. While adopting the reading *Kyrne* "sans grande conviction," Van Groningen (82) remarks, "la psychologie y est d'une confusion remarquable." *Thyme* was

probably written in the archetype of our manuscript tradition; but I think Theognis said, *"Kyrne."*

4. The transmitted text of the following line seems to be hopelessly corrupt. It seems to say: "for the sake of the other, courted sea voyage."

Selected Bibliography

Introduction

Budge, W. *By Nile and Tigris*. London: J. Murray, 1920.

Cook, J.M. "Greek Settlement of the Eastern Aegean and Asia Minor." *Cambridge Ancient History* 2.2 (1975): 773–804.

———. "Old Smyrna, 1948–1951." *The Annual of the British School at Athens* 53 (1958): 1–34.

Graham, A.J. "The Expansion of the Greek World, Eighth to Sixth Centuries B.C." *Cambridge Ancient History* 3.3 (1982): 83–162.

Hammond, N. "History of the Middle East and the Aegean Region c. 1380–1000 B.C." *Cambridge Ancient History* 2.2 (1975): 678–712.

Havelock, E.A. *The Literate Revolution in Greece and Its Cultural Consequences*. Princeton: Princeton University Press, 1982.

Isserlin, B.S.J. "The Antiquity of the Greek Alphabet." *Kadmos* 22 (1983): 151–63.

Jeffery, L.H. *The Local Scripts of Archaic Greece*. London: Oxford University Press, 1961.

Powell, B.B. "Why was the Greek Alphabet Invented? The Epigraphical Evidence." *Classical Antiquity* 8.2 (October 1989): 321–50.

Smith, S. "The Greek Trade at Al Mina." *The Antiquaries Journal* 22.2 (April 1942): 87–112.

Snodgrass, A. *Archaic Greece*. London: J.M. Dent, 1980.

Wade-Gery, H.T. *The Poet of the Iliad*. Cambridge: Cambridge University Press, 1952.

West, M.L. *Greek Metre*. London: Oxford University Press, 1982.

Translations

The Oxyrhynchus Papyri. Vol. 1 (Sappho fragment 3), B.P. Grenfell and A.S. Hunt. London: Egypt Exploration Fund, 1898. Vol. 10 (Alcaeus fragments 3–6), B.P. Grenfell and A.S. Hunt. London: Egypt Exploration Fund, 1914. Vol. 15 (Alcaeus fragment 1, Ibycus fragment 1), B.P. Grenfell and A.S. Hunt. London: Egypt Exploration Society, 1922. Vol. 17 (Ibycus fragment 1), A.S. Hunt. London: Egypt Exploration Society, 1927. Vol. 18 (Alcaeus fragments 7–8), E. Lobel, C.H. Roberts, and E.P. Wegener. London: Egypt Exploration Society, 1941. Vol. 21 (Alcaeus fragment 2), E.

Lobel. London: Egypt Exploration Society, 1951. Vol. 22 (Archilochus frag-
ment 3), E. Lobel and C.H. Roberts. London: Egypt Exploration Society,
1954. Vol. 24 (Alcman fragment 1), E. Lobel, C.H. Roberts, E.G. Turner,
and J.W.B. Barns. London: Egypt Exploration Society, 1957. Vol. 32 (Stesi-
chorus fragment 2), E. Lobel. London: Egypt Exploration Society, 1967.

Barnestone, W. *Sappho and the Greek Lyric Poets*. New York: Schocken
Books, 1988.

Barron, J.P. "Ibycus: to Polycrates." *London University Institute of Classical
Studies Bulletin* 16 (1969): 118–49.

Bollack, J., P.J. de la Combe, and H. Wiseman. "La replique de Jocaste."
Cahiers de Philologie 2. Lille: Publications de l' Université de Lille, 1977.

Bowra, C. *Pindar: The Odes*. London: Penguin, 1969.

Bremer, J.M., A.M. van Erp Taalman Kip, and S.R. Slings. *Some Recently
Found Greek Poems*. Leiden: E.J. Brill, 1987.

Campbell, D.A. *Greek Lyric Poetry*. Bristol: Bristol Classical Press, 1982.

———. *Greek Lyric I: Sappho, Alcaeus*. Cambridge, Mass.: Harvard University
Press, 1982.

———. *Greek Lyric II: Anacreon, Anacreontea, Choral Lyric from Olympus to
Alcman*. Cambridge, Mass.: Harvard University Press, 1989.

Carey, C. *A Commentary on Five Odes of Pindar*. New York: Arno Press, 1981.

Diehl, E. *Anthologia Lyrica Graeca: Fasc. 1, Poetae Elegiaci*. Leipzig: Teubner,
1954.

———. *Anthologia Lyrica Graeca: Fasc. 3, Iamborum Scriptores*. Leipzig:
Teubner, 1954.

Diels, H. and W. Kranz. *Die Fragmente der Vorsokratiker*. Berlin: Weidmann,
1951.

Edmonds, J.M. *Elegy and Iambus I*. Cambridge, Mass.: Harvard University
Press, 1931.

———. *Elegy and Iambus II*. Cambridge, Mass.: Harvard University Press,
1928.

Farnell, L. *Critical Commentary to the Works of Pindar*. Amsterdam: Adolf M.
Hakkert, 1961.

Gerber, D. *Pindar's Olympian One: A Commentary*. Toronto: University of
Toronto Press, 1982.

Gentili, B. *Anacreon*. Rome: Athenaeum, 1958.

Gentili, B. and C. Prato *Poetarum Elegiacorum Testimonia et Fragmenta*. Leipzig:
Teubner, 1979.

Kirkwood, G. *Selections From Pindar*. Chico, Cal.: Scholars Press, 1982.

Linforth, I.M. *Solon the Athenian*. Berkeley: University of California Press,
1919.

Lloyd-Jones, H. *Females of the Species: Semonides on Women*. London: Duck-
worth, 1975.

Lobel, E. "Corinna." *Hermes* 65 (1930): 356–65.

Lobel, E. and D. Page. *Poetarum Lesbiorum Fragmenta*. London: Oxford Uni-
versity Press, 1955.

Maehler, H. *Die Lieder des Bakchylides: I. Die* Siegeslieder. Leiden: Brill, 1982.

Page, D.L. *Alcman: the Partheneion.* London: Oxford University Press, 1951.

———. *Corinna.* London: Society for the Promotion of Hellenistic Studies, 1963.

———. *Poetae Melici Graeci.* London: Oxford University Press, 1962.

———. *Sappho and Alcaeus.* London: Oxford University Press, 1955.

———. *Supplementum Lyricis Graecis.* London: Oxford University Press, 1974.

Podlecki, A.J. *The Early Greek Poets and Their Times.* Vancouver: University of British Columbia Press, 1984.

Snell, B. and H. Maehler. *Bacchylidis Carmina Cum Fragmentis.* Leipzig: Teubner, 1970.

Swanson, R.A. *Pindar's Odes.* Indianopolis: Bobbs-Merrill, 1974.

Van Groningen, B.A. *Theognis: Le Premier Livre.* Amsterdam: Nord-Hollandische Uitgevers Maatschappij, 1966.

Voigt, E. *Sappho and Alcaeus:* Fragmenta. Amsterdam: Athenaeum-Polak & Van Gennep, 1971.

West, M.L. "Alcmanica." *Classical Quarterly* n.s. 15 (1965): 194–202.

———. *Iambi et Elegi Graeci II.* London: Oxford University Press, 1972.

———. *Iambi et Elegi Graeci I: Editio Altera.* London: Oxford University Press, 1989.

Wilamowitz-Moellendorff, U. v. *Pindaros.* Berlin: Weidmann, 1966. Originally published 1922.

Winnington-Ingram, R. "Pindar's Ninth Pythian Ode." *Bulletin of the Institute of Classical Studies* 16 (1969): 9–15.

Woodbury, L. "Apollo's First Love: Pindar, Pyth. 9.26 ff." *Transactions of the American Philological Association* 103 (1972): 561–73.

Index

Ann Arbor Paperbacks